# Literature in Perspective

Of recent years, the ordinary man who reads for pleasure has been gradually excluded from that great debate in which every intelligent reader of the classics takes part. There are two reasons for this: first, so much criticism floods from the world's presses that no one but a scholar living entirely among books can hope to read it all; and second, the critics and analysts, mostly academics, use a language that only their fellows in the same discipline can understand.

Consequently criticism, which should be as 'inevitable as breathing'—an activity for which we are all qualified—has become the private field of a few warring factions who shout their unintelligible battle cries to each other but make little communication to the common man.

*Literature in Perspective* aims at giving a straightforward account of literature and of writers—straightforward both in content and in language. Critical jargon is as far as possible avoided; any terms that must be used are explained simply; and the constant preoccupation of the authors of the Series is to be lucid.

It is our hope that each book will be easily understood, that it will adequately describe its subject without pretentiousness so that the intelligent reader who wants to know about Donne or Keats or Thackeray will find enough in it to bring him up to date on critical estimates.

Even those who are well read, we believe, can benefit from a lucid exposition of what they may have taken for granted, and perhaps—dare it be said?—not fully understood.

K. H. G.

5

# Thackeray

During the last ten years of his life and for some time after his death, Thackeray's reputation stood extremely high. In 1857 George Eliot said that she thought of him, '. . . as I suppose the majority of people with any intellect do, as on the whole the most powerful of living novelists'. In 1867 Walter Bagehot wrote:

> Of Thackeray it is too early to speak at length. A certain distance is needful for a just criticism. The present generation have learned too much from him to be able to judge him rightly.
>
> OF STERNE AND THACKERAY

The reassessment which Bagehot wanted has never come about. After the initial decline in reputation which usually follows great contemporary success Thackeray has not met with consistent and objective critical examination and has too often been made the butt of critical theorists, belittled because he did not write like Henry James or condemned out of hand by those who thought it enough to label him a sentimentalist and leave it at that. The present study cannot attempt to be a reassessment, though there are signs that the time for it is not far distant. This book is no more than an introduction, which will have fulfilled its aim if it be found to be objective in its approach and helpful to those readers who want the material to make their own evaluation of an author whose status has yet to be fairly considered and truly ascertained.

I. M. W.

Literature in Perspective

# Thackeray

Ioan M. Williams WITHDRAWN

Evans Brothers Limited, London

Published by Evans Brothers Limited
Montague House, Russell Square, London, W.C.1
© Ioan M. Williams 1968
First published 1968

Set in 11 on 12 point Bembo and printed in Great Britain
by The Camelot Press Ltd., London and Southampton
237    44460    7 cased                    PR4459
237    44472    0 limp

# 19481

## LUTON SIXTH FORM COLLEGE

| | | |
|---|---|---|
| -6. NOV. 1973 | | |
| -1 APR. 1974 | | |
| 2?. APR. 1974 | | |
| -7 MAY 1974 | | |
| -7 JUN 1974 | | |
| | | |
| | | |
| | | |
| | | |

This book is due for return on or before the last date shown above.

Literature in Perspective

General Editor: Kenneth H. Grose

WITHDRAWN

# Thackeray

# Contents

# The Author

Ioan M. Williams, B.A., B.Litt., is Lecturer in English at the University of Warwick.

# Acknowledgements

The author and publishers are indebted to Mrs. Robert Dickinson and Mrs. Edward Norman-Butler for their kind permission to reproduce the portrait of Thackeray by Samuel Laurence on the cover of this book.

Volume and page references to Thackeray's works are to the Smith, Elder *Biographical Edition* (13 volumes, 1898–9).

# I

# The Early Years of a 'Week-day Preacher'

William Makepeace Thackeray was a satirist and a sentiment-alist; with piercing sharpness of vision he revealed the inevitable pressure of selfishness behind human thought and action but always insisted on the power and goodness of human feeling. After he had published *Vanity Fair* and become famous for the first time in a long career, he paused in his creative writing to describe the qualities of certain English writers who had preceded him and in doing so he described his own position. His *Lectures on the English Humourists . . .* (1852) contain subjective assessments of Swift, Congreve, Addison, Steele, Prior, Gay, Pope, Hogarth, Smollett, Fielding, Sterne and Goldsmith, valuable now mainly because they tell us what Thackeray thought about the 18th century and show his expanded definition of humour.

From these lectures and from his comments elsewhere we learn that Thackeray was basically suspicious of the effects of satire. Once in his letters he suggested that laughter itself is 'of the deevil'; he disliked Byron's *Don Juan* and thought Swift:

> . . . a vast genius, a magnificent genius, a genius wonderfully bright, and dazzling, and strong,—to seize, to know, to see, to flash upon falsehood and scorch it into perdition, to penetrate into the hidden motives, and expose the black thoughts of men,—an awful, an evil spirit.
>
> Lecture on Swift VII, 441

For Thackeray Steele was the most attractive of the writers with whom he was concerned because he 'came down into common life' and showed, if not the greatest brilliance or power of intellect, the strongest vein of human feeling. Humour, as he defined it, involved laughter, but appealed to tears, striving towards what George Meredith called 'the embrace of contrasts'. At the beginning of his lecture on Swift he wrote:

> If Humour only meant laughter, you would scarcely feel more interest about humorous writers than about the private life of poor Harlequin . . . who possesses in common with these the power of making you laugh. . . . The humorous writer professes to awaken and direct your love, your pity, your kindness—your scorn for untruth, pretention, imposture—your tenderness for the weak, the poor, the oppressed, the unhappy. To the best of his means and ability he comments on all the ordinary actions and passions of life almost. He takes upon himself to be the week-day preacher, so to speak.                  Lecture on Swift VII, 423–4

This passage describes the image which, in his mature years, Thackeray tried to project, objecting strenuously to charges of cynicism and never more pleased than when his readers saw under the satirical mask a sentimental gentleman.

Thackeray was an uncompromising realist, objecting to idealisation and exaggeration alike. When David Masson wrote a review in which he closely compared Thackeray with his contemporary and rival for public esteem, Charles Dickens, Thackeray took the opportunity of writing to him and making a fundamental statement of theory. Of Dickens he said:

> I quarrel with his Art in many respects: w^h I don't think represents Nature duly; for instance Micawber appears to me an exaggeration of a man as his name is of a name. It is delightful and makes me laugh: but it is no more a real man than my friend Punch is: and in so far I protest against him . . . holding that the Art of Novels *is* to represent Nature: to convey as strongly as possible the sentiment of reality. . . .             Letter to Masson, 6 May 1851

This standard of realism Thackeray applied unremittingly to his own work and that of other novelists which he happened to review, but it did not prevent him from giving full measure of praise to what he felt was Dickens's greatest quality. The last of his first series of lectures he concludes with a tribute to this effect:

> I may quarrel with Mr. Dickens's art a thousand and a thousand times, I delight and wonder at his genius; I recognise in it—I speak with awe and reverence—a commission from that Divine Benefi-

cence, whose blessed task we know it will one day be to wipe every tear from every eye. Thankfully I take my share of the feast of love and kindness which this gentle, and generous, and charitable soul has contributed to the happiness of the world. I take and enjoy my share, and say a Benediction for the meal. CHARITY AND HUMOUR VII, 725

The attempt to attain this quality himself and to reconcile it with his function of social criticism and moral realism dominated Thackeray's later years.

This position was not, however, reached at once. Thackeray's early work reflects a slow process of development by which he achieved the reconciliation of satire and sentiment. Thackeray himself saw the development as the result of increasing age and the growth of family responsibilities. He wrote to a young friend in 1849:

I suppose we all begin so [i.e. too 'savage']—I know one who did: and who is sorry now for pelting at that poor old Bulwer & others, but it was in the days of hot youth when I was scarcely older than you are now.        Letter to James Hannay, 29 June 1849

At about this time in his life he came to regret many of the tendencies in his early work and took several opportunities to emphasise his change of mind. The kind of thing which he regretted is shown most clearly in his treatment of the work of Bulwer Lytton.

POOR OLD BULWER

Edward George Lytton Bulwer (1803–73), politician and diplomat, first Baron Lytton, was a voluminous novelist and poet, an author of considerable importance in his own right. He wrote no single work which achieved major status but is remembered by the reading public today as the author of *Harold* and *The Last Days of Pompeii*. He is of interest also in that he is the most substantial representative of a type of novelist important throughout the 19th century and dominant in England during the years immediately after the death of Sir Walter Scott, one of the first writers of the period to give close attention to questions of technique in novel-writing, and reflects in his long career many of the major changes that affected fiction between 1830 and 1870.

Bulwer Lytton was primarily the exponent of Idealism in the novel. He made a combination of ideas drawn from German romantic thought and a vaguely conceived Platonism which he applied in defence of a series of novels which represented what, in Thackeray's estimation, was a gross distortion of reality. Thackeray read Lytton's earlier novels without feeling a great deal of antagonism. He recorded in his diary his reading of *The Disowned* (1828), and *Devereux* (1829), commenting on the latter:

> I do not admire *Devereux* as a whole so much as either of the other two novels of Mr. Bulwer's, I think he has taken more pains about it than either, it is full of thoughts strong and deep, but he has strung his pearls on a poor & fragile thread, the story is I think the most miserable composition, I could write as good a one myself. . . .
>
> Letter to his Mother, 2 September 1829

His attitude was not fully formulated until the appearance of Lytton's *Eugene Aram* in 1832. This novel, an example of the type known and attacked at the time as 'Newgate fiction', elevated to the status of hero a murderer whose crime was recorded in the notorious *Newgate Calendar*. By 1832 Thackeray had had ample opportunity to read and assimilate the work of Thomas Carlyle, whose early essays and *Sartor Resartus* (1833–4) made a violent and impressive attack on sham sentiment and cant in general and on Bulwer Lytton in particular. His hostility strengthened by his reading of Carlyle, Thackeray dismissed *Eugene Aram* as 'humbug' and joined the staff of *Fraser's Magazine* (where Carlyle's work was appearing) in a concentrated attack against everything which Lytton's novels stood for.

The best known and most brilliant attack on Bulwer Lytton which Thackeray ever made was the parody which he published in his series of *Novels by Eminent Hands* in *Punch* (1847), but his early work contains many attacks on 'poor old Bulwer's' style, subject-matter and personality. Later in his career, when his mood had changed and when Bulwer's writings had become more realistic, Thackeray regretted the violence of these attacks and made a personal apology to the subject of them. But in the early years of his career as miscellaneous writer, reviewer, sub-editor and foreign correspondent, his attitude to the more established writer was, by his own confession, typical of his lighthearted and primarily satiric outlook.

## THACKERAY'S EARLY LIFE

The change in Thackeray's attitude which took place in the later 1840s has been attributed to a change in his external circumstances; and to some extent this is true, the shape of his whole career having been affected by events which occurred between his birth in 1811 and the virtual loss of his wife in 1841.

Thackeray's father, Richmond Thackeray, was the prosperous and efficient servant of the East India Company, at that time responsible for the government of the greater part of the Indian sub-continent. His mother, Anne Becher, came from a family which had a tradition of service in India and it was there that she met and married Richmond Thackeray. Their son was born in Calcutta and lived there until after the death of his father in September 1815. In December 1816 he was sent to England to receive his education, arrived there in May 1817 and was sent to school in Southampton.

From Southampton, where he was badly treated, Thackeray was sent to a school in Chiswick run by a cousin of his mother, and went from there in July 1822 to attend Charterhouse School as a boarder. Meanwhile, in March 1817, his mother had married Major-General Carmichael Smythe, an officer whom she had known and loved before she met Richmond Thackeray and whom she would have married before going to India if she had not been deceived by her family, who had told her that he was dead.

Thackeray's experiences at the various schools he attended, and particularly at Charterhouse, are an important part of his biography. In later years his attitude towards them changed, but for the greater part of his life he referred to Charterhouse as Slaughterhouse and frequently inveighed against the kind of learning which he was forced to attempt, the brutality and callousness of his teachers and the immorality and vice which flourished in the underorganised and brutal school system. In 1844 he reviewed Dean Stanley's life of Dr. Thomas Arnold, headmaster of Rugby and famous for his attempt to impose on his school a Christian discipline, and he wrote:

> Every man whose own school-days are not very distant, and who can remember that strange ordeal of his early life—the foolish old-world superstitions which obtained in the public school; the wretched portion of letters meted out to him there—the misery, vice, and folly, which were taught along with the small share of Greek and Latin imparted to him—the ten years wasted in the pursuit of a couple of languages which not one lad in a hundred mastered —the total ignorance upon all other matters of learning, which was almost enjoined by the public school system—will be apt to think, as we imagine, Why had I not Arnold for a master?'
>
> MORNING CHRONICLE, 3 JUNE 1844

Thackeray's unhappiness under the system so described was increased when he came higher up the school and under the immediate authority of the headmaster, Dr. Russell, who seems to have taken a particular dislike to him and to have treated him with consistent brutality. When he left Charterhouse in May 1828 Thackeray's predominant feeling was one of relief.

After a short time spent with his mother and stepfather at Larkebeare in Devon, and an illness which kept him in bed for some months, Thackeray took up residence in Trinity College, Cambridge, in February 1929. He stayed in Cambridge only until July 1830, by that time convinced that he was not to meet with any substantial academic success. While there he formed several friendships which were to last him a lifetime—particularly that with Edward FitzGerald, now remembered as the translator of *Omar Khayyam*—took part in the activities of several societies, made sporadic attempts to master Greek and algebra, and wrote for the undergraduate publications—*The Snob* and *The Gownsman*—a series of contributions which gave no indications of outstanding ability. When he left Cambridge it was after some discussion with his mother and stepfather, who were most concerned about his future, that he went for several months to Germany, with the intention of broadening his experience of the world and preparing himself for a regular occupation.

After travelling for a time Thackeray settled in Weimar,

famous for some years past as a centre of German culture and the home of Goethe, Wieland and Schiller. When Thackeray visited Weimar, Schiller and Wieland were dead, but he met Goethe and formed one of the circle of young Englishmen and Frenchmen who gathered around his daughter-in-law, Ottilie von Goethe, contributing to her cosmopolitan magazine *Das Chaos*. Partly in fun and partly seriously, Thackeray twice fell in love at Weimar, to be twice disillusioned and to return home in a mood of mingled sadness and amusement, like an early type of one of his own narrators.

In May 1831 the visit to Germany was over and Thackeray had returned to England to begin studying law. How seriously he ever intended to apply himself is doubtful; his letters to Edward FitzGerald and to his mother show that he very quickly became bored with this pursuit and reacted strongly against the apparent pointlessness of the enforced mode of study. The next few years of his life saw the abandonment of the attempt on law and the adoption of several other methods of acquiring occupation and fortune. In July 1832 Thackeray reached his majority and spent a period of four months in Paris. By January 1833 he had tried bill-broking as a profession; later that year he had determined to cultivate the talent for drawing which he had shown very early in his life and to train as a professional artist. By September 1834, after some months in London with his mother and stepfather, he was settled in Paris, living with his grandmother, going to the theatre, writing and attending an atelier as an art student. It was during this period that he met and fell in love with Isabel Shawe.

Isabel Shawe also had connections with the Indian service. Her father had been an officer of the East India Company and died on service in 1826. After his death Mrs. Shawe retired to Paris, where she kept five children on a very narrow income. The experience seems to have soured her temper and brought her to a neurotic condition. Her behaviour to Thackeray, before and after his marriage, was viciously selfish and self-deceived, and was a major source of pain and anxiety to him. Mrs. Shawe, at first not unfavourable to the relationship, later opposed it, working on the personality of a daughter who at nineteen was immature and weak-minded, with no idea of the responsibilities involved in a mature relationship. But Isabel loved Thackeray enough to respond to his attempts to free her from her mother's influence and they were married in Paris on 20 August 1836.

The first years of the marriage were happy ones. At first they lived in Paris, but moved to London in March 1837, where their first two children were born—Anne in June 1837, Jane in July 1838. Unfortunately the second daughter died after eight months and when the third daughter, Harriet, was born in May 1840, Isabel sunk into a depression which was partly the result of the earlier loss. Exactly what caused the illness which followed is uncertain, but in the months after Harriet's birth Isabel's depression grew deeper, centring on feelings of inadequacy as a wife and mother. To some extent the powerful influence of Mrs. Carmichael Smythe, acting on Isabel's feelings of guilt about not being able to manage a household, and Thackeray's style of living which involved silence and consideration at home and constant resource to the stimulus of company outside the home, were contributory factors. Recent biographers have freed Thackeray from any responsibility for what happened—he did everything that he could to avert the illness once he became aware of its extent and tendency—but the circumstances which he, as a vigorous but overworked writer, required in order to meet his engagements and keep the family helped to make Isabel feel that she was excluded from his life, inadequate and an encumbrance rather than a companion.

Whatever the causes for her condition, it soon became painfully and dramatically evident that Isabel was insane. A journey to Ireland which Thackeray and the family took in September 1840 brought the matter to a head. On the sea journey Isabel attempted suicide several times. In Ireland, where they had gone to meet her mother and sister, her condition worsened and the vicious neuroticism of Mrs. Shawe made the situation unbearable for Thackeray. In October they returned to England, the daughters were put in the care of Mrs. Carmichael Smythe, and from time to time during the next few years Thackeray took Isabel to one doctor and another in the hope of obtaining a cure.

By 1846 it was evident that her insanity was incurable; she was consigned to the care of an attendant, in whose charge she remained, outliving her husband by thirty years.

So, from 1841, Thackeray was as much alone as he had been in his earliest years, but now with the responsibility of a family. Before Isabel's illness some six years of ceaseless activity seemed to be leading to a measure of success and financial security, but the upheaval which that event brought about retarded his progress for some time. The years of his marriage had been years of comparative poverty. The fortune which his father left and which should have been enough to provide Thackeray with a comfortable living was dissipated by 1833. Exactly how it went is uncertain. Thackeray himself, as a result of the passion for gambling which he acquired during his visits to Paris as an undergraduate in 1829 and 1830, disposed of at least £2,000. While he was at Cambridge he was selected for treatment by two professional gamblers who deprived him of £1,500, which he paid when he came of age. Before he lost the habit it cost him other large sums —100 guineas in December 1831, £600 in February 1833. Yet these losses seem to have left the greater part of his fortune untouched, and it was not until after the Indian banking crisis of 1830–4 that he was left with only £7,000 out of the £17,000 which he had received from his father. Out of this sum annuities amounting to £277 a year had to be paid; so he was left with the choice of using his slender capital or living on an income of something around £100 a year. In view of this he and his stepfather, General Carmichael Smythe, attempted to obtain a controlling influence in a newspaper which would allow a regular and sufficient income to Thackeray as editor or foreign correspondent. As early as April 1832 Thackeray had been involved in some unsuccessful negotiations to buy a newspaper. In January 1833 he acquired an interest in the *National Standard* and *Journal of Literature, Science, Music and the Fine Arts*, writing for it until May of that year and then acting as editor and proprietor. In February 1834, however, the paper failed and it was not until 1836 that Thackeray became involved with another paper.

In that year a company directed by General Carmichael Smythe was set up to acquire and direct a new radical newspaper—the result was the *Constitutional and Public Ledger*, which appeared from 15 September 1836 and for which Thackeray acted as Paris Correspondent at a salary of £400 a year, on which he married Isabel Shawe. Their return to England in March 1837 was largely the result of the *Constitutional*'s financial difficulties, which Thackeray attempted to solve when he was made editor in April of that year. His efforts, however, were in vain, and the paper ceased publication in July, leaving both him and his stepfather with financial liabilities which were not settled for several years to come.

During the years between 1830 and 1844, under the pressure of financial necessity and the need to acquire reputation, Thackeray contributed articles, reviews, sketches and stories to over twenty-four newspapers, magazines and periodicals, ranging in status from *The Times* and *The Morning Chronicle* to the *Comic Almanack* and the *Corsair*. He acted as editor to at least three newspapers, *The National Standard*, *The Constitutional* and *Galignani's Messenger*, the last a Paris composition. He applied for posts as foreign correspondent to various London papers, acted as such for the two with which he was financially concerned and tried his hand as an illustrator, applying to Dickens for the job of illustrating *Pickwick Papers*. Throughout the period he contributed to *Fraser's Magazine* and at the end of it he began the association with the recently founded *Punch*, which brought him more pay and a better reputation than any of his other connections. From 1830–44 was a period of incessant activity, while he struggled for financial security and literary reputation.

It was partly a natural result of his being allied to no group and having no fixed place in society that Thackeray became a social critic. From Bohemia, the disreputable, classless and lively society of London journalism and night life, he could look at society objectively. The innate tendency to criticism which he noted in his diary as early as 1832:

> I have become much more worldly & far less open to enthusiasm—not relishing poetry as I used or fancied I used—If I live to fifty I dare say I shall be as cold-blooded & calculating as the worst of them.   DIARY, 28 JUNE 1832

was probably increased by his reading of the work of Thomas Carlyle and by his friendship with William Maginn, the rebellious editor of *Fraser's Magazine* and the most fiery and irresponsible of critics. On the other hand, it is important to see the connection between his satire and criticism and the early idealism which is suggested in the passage quoted above. If in 1832 when he was insecure, energetic and a little bitter, Thackeray was to become primarily a satirist, it is important to remember that his early life, his loneliness and later deprivations had deeply impressed on him the value of the domestic virtues, of love and of purity of heart.

THE REAL AND THE IDEAL

Three minor works of Thackeray give important indications of the source of his creative impulse. Throughout his life he loved the theatre; as a boy he had been entranced by the world of sublime passion and beauty which it revealed to him. His first published book was *Flore et Zephyr* (1836), in which, by illustrations, he parodied the ballet of Taglione and suggested a reality of ugliness behind the ideal grace of the dancer (see illustrations). In his youth, and throughout his life, he admired and read the novels and romances of Sir Walter Scott. *Ivanhoe* in particular represented for him the beauty of romance. Yet in 1850 he published *Rebecca and Rowena or Romance upon Romance*, a satirical continuation of Scott's story, which grew out of his preference for the Jewess Rebecca rather than the Saxon Rowena, but which had the effect of deflating the whole idea of heroic romance, bringing into light the reality of war and female selfishness. The story ends with the marriage of Ivanhoe and Rebecca, but even in its ending deflates the idea of the 'happiness for ever after':

> That she and Ivanhoe were married, follows of course; . . . Married I am sure they were, and adopted little Cedric; but I don't think they had any other children, or were subsequently very boisterously happy. Of some sort of happiness melancholy is a characteristic, and I think these were a solemn pair, and died rather early.
>
> REBECCA AND ROWENA IX, 158

More important in Thackeray's life even than the influence of romance was his admiration for female affection, the dedicated love which woman can give to man. Yet in 1843, in *Fraser's Magazine*, he published *Bluebeard's Ghost*, a skit which begins with a penetrating satire on the source of female affection. The story of Bluebeard is well known—he had married a young wife, was kind to her in all ways, but laid an injunction on her never to enter a certain room on pain of death. Curiosity overcomes fear and Mrs. Bluebeard enters the room—to find there the embalmed corpses of seven predecessors. Bluebeard returns, discovers her disobedience and is about to murder her when, as the result of the quick thinking of her younger sister, she is saved by her brothers, who kill her husband. Thackeray's story begins after the death of Bluebeard. The latter part of the story is not important, but the opening scene depicts a savagely comic argument between Mrs. Bluebeard and her sister. The former has forgotten the real nature of the circumstances which caused her husband's death, has deceived herself and become a pattern widow:

> For some time after the fatal accident which deprived her of her husband, Mrs. Bluebeard was, as may be imagined, in a state of profound grief.
>
> There was not a widow in all the country who went to such an expense for black bombazeen.      BLUEBEARD'S GHOST XIII, 508

The widow quarrels with her sister over the latter's refusal to wear mourning:

> 'I will never wear mourning for that odious wretch, sister!' Anne would cry.
>
> 'I will trouble you, Miss Anne, not to use such words in my presence regarding the best of husbands, or to quit the room at once!' the widow would answer.
>
> 'I'm sure it's no great pleasure to sit in it. I wonder you don't make use of the closet, sister, where the *other* Mrs. Bluebeards are.'
>
> 'Impertinence! they were all embalmed by Monsieur Gannal. How dare you report the monstrous calumnies regarding the best of men? Take down the family Bible and read what my blessed saint says of his wives—read it written in his own hand:—
>
> ' "Friday, June 20.—Married my beloved wife, Anna Maria Scrogginsia.
>
> "Saturday, August 1.—A bereaved husband has scarcely strength

to write down in this chronicle that the dearest of wives, Anna Maria Scrogginsia, expired this day of sore throat". . . .'

BLUEBEARD'S GHOST XIII, 509

None of these three stories would have a place in a selection of the best of Thackeray's work, but all show quite clearly the relation between sentimental attraction and satirical attack, and indicate that his realistic deflation was a reaction against the objects of youthful and idealistic enthusiasm.

Perhaps the most important single factor in Thackeray's development as a critic of society and an analyst of human motivation was his relationship with his mother. Deprived of her love at an early age, he prayed while at school at Southampton that he should be able to dream of her. When he met her again he was overwhelmed by her presence. Yet as he grew older he had to reconcile himself with her second marriage, with the possessiveness of her love and with the fact that she was not as devoted as her emotional demands would imply. He described this process himself:

> When I was a boy at Larkebeare, I thought her an Angel & worshipped her. I see but a woman now, O so tender so loving so cruel.
> Letter to Mary Holmes, 25 February 1852

His relationship with his mother was not unusually close, or her love for him excessive, but as he grew older it became the focal point of the feelings of disillusionment which he associated with the process of growing up. Working on a nature always sensitive to the impressions involved in human relationships, these feelings of disillusionment combined with the 'spirit of the Age' and the influence of writers like Thomas Carlyle to make Thackeray a realist and a satirist and to produce a tension within him which resulted in a subtle and powerful conception of social relationships and human behaviour. This did not, however, happen at once, and it is in his early stories that we see Thackeray working towards the maturity of technique and perception which was not completely achieved until he had served an apprenticeship of fifteen years and assumed the garb of the 'week-day preacher'.

# 2

# Savage Beginnings

We do not know when Thackeray first began to contribute
regularly to *Fraser's Magazine*, the outspoken and aggressively
lively magazine of the 1830s. His first major contribution, *The
Yellowplush Papers*, appeared between November 1837 and July
1838, but it seems that he had been a contributor for some time
before that. His introduction to the magazine, for which he produced most of his work during the years between 1837 and 1844,
when he transferred his allegiance to the recently formed *Punch*,
was probably through his friendship with the editor, William
Maginn. According to Francis Mahony, ex-Jesuit scholar and
journalist who wrote under the name of Father Prout, Thackeray
met Maginn some time in 1832. The cause of the meeting seems
to have been Thackeray's desire to begin a newspaper and his
need for the assistance of someone like Maginn who could give
him advice and guidance. A certain sum of money passed from
Thackeray to Maginn for his services, perhaps with the short-
lived *National Standard*. Their relationship seems also to have led
to collaboration on articles for *Fraser's*, but it was not until 1837
that any work appeared in the magazine which was recognisable
as by Thackeray writing alone and of sufficient quality to be
considered important.

'THE MEMOIRS OF C. J. YELLOWPLUSH SOMETIME FOOTMAN IN MANY
GENTEEL FAMILIES'
Thackeray first presented Charles Yellowplush to the public in a
review of J. H. Skelton's *My Book, or, The Anatomy of Conduct*,
which he entitled *Fashnable Fax and Polite Annygoats*, but the
character, beyond his snobbishness and mixture of affected

speech with Cockney dialect, was not developed until the second paper, *Miss Shum's Husband*, in which he informs us of his birth and early education. Yellowplush is a rogue, at first naïve and deserving of some sympathy, but later ignorant, cunning and a servile worshipper of rank and self-interest.

The story deals with Yellowplush's experience in his first situation, as servant to Mr. Frederick Altamont, a gentlemanly crossing-sweeper who keeps the secret of his occupation from the weak-minded though affectionate wife whom he has rescued from the persecutions of a vulgar, snobbish and overbearing family of stepmother and stepsisters. The secrecy is too much for her; worked on by her relations and stimulated by ideas of mystery and horror drawn from bad novels, she pursues him to the City, learns his secret and is horrified at the vulgarity of his occupation. Altamont sells his place outside the Bank and they retire on his savings to the Continent. The story is a fairly light-hearted one, directed partly against the vulgar snobbishness of the wife's family, partly against the foolishness of a society in which gentility depends on the nature of one's occupation, and partly against Charles himself, who reveals his own ignorance and shallow-mindedness during the course of the narration. The next incident, *Dimond cut Dimond*, is concerned with two rogues —the fashionable and coldly selfish Algernon Deuceace and the blustering but relatively simple-minded Richard Blewitt—who first quarrel over and then conspire to cheat the unsuspecting dupe, Mr. Dawkins. When this is done, however, the superior duplicity of Deuceace reveals itself; he refuses to share the takings with his fellow conspirator and departs for France—leaving his laundress's bill unpaid.

The third and longest of the stories is concerned with the adventures of master and servant in Paris. Here, armed with the £5,000 which he won from Dawkins, the Honourable Algernon Deuceace fixes on a couple of ladies living together on an income of £9,000 per annum. He succeeds in attracting the regard of the frigid Lady Griffin, widow of the defunct Lieutenant-General Sir George Griffin, K.C.B.!, and in gaining the adoration of her sentimental, hunchbacked stepdaughter. Having proceeded thus far he is unable to decide which one to propose marriage to. The daughter is of age, but the stepmother controls the fortune; and before he can make a decision he has to discover what would happen to the money in the event of the girl's marriage, meanwhile playing one woman against the other.

The affair is at this delicate point when the unexpected arrival of Deuceace's father, the Earl of Crabs, throws his son into confusion. The scene containing the meeting of father and son is a brilliant exposure of selfishness and cold-hearted duplicity on both sides. By the end of the first interview it is clear that the issue of the action will depend on which of the two is the bigger rogue—the focus of the story shifts to the battle which results from Deuceace's refusal to give his father £1,000 out of his winnings and so stave off an arrest for debt which the elder has left England to avoid. As it develops, the story becomes an exposure of frigidity and malice on all sides. Deuceace is deceived by Lady Griffin into declaring himself in favour of the daughter. Her attraction for him turns to hatred, she forces him into a duel in which he loses his left hand and aided by his father, she buys up his debts, obtains his imprisonment and thus compels him to use his £5,000 to settle them. As the action proceeds it becomes clear that the criterion for success in the world which the characters have created for themselves is the degree of self-control with which they implement their selfish ends. This is a world in which emotional involvement is fatal. Yellowplush comments on his master's anger:

And this I've perseaved in the cors of my expearants through life, that when you vex him, a roag's no longer a roag: you find him out at onst when he's in a passion, for he shows, as it ware, his cloven foot the very instnt you tread on it. At least, this is what *young* roags do; it requires very cool blood and long practis to get over this pint, and not to show your pashn when you feel it and snarl when you are angry. . . . And it's also to be remarked (a very profownd observatin for a footmin, but we have i's though we *do* wear plush britchis), it's to be remarked, I say, that one of these chaps is much sooner maid angry than another, because honest men yield to other people, roags never do; honest men love other people, roags only themselves; and the slightest thing which comes in the way of thir beloved objects sets them fewrious. Master hadn't led a life of gambling, swindling, and every kind of debotch to be good-tempered at the end of it, I prommis you.

THE AMOURS OF MR. DEUCEACE III, 306

The Earl of Crabs is an entirely superior rogue:

He'd got to that pitch that he didn't mind injaries—they were all fair play to him—he gave 'em and reseav'd them, without a thought of mallis. If he wanted to injer his son, it was to benefick himself.                    THE AMOURS OF MR. DEUCEACE III, 323

It soon becomes apparent that, pitted against such an opponent, Algernon Deuceace has little chance of success. He frees himself from prison and succeeds in marrying the daughter, under the impression that she is the heiress, but when he returns from the honeymoon he discovers that his father has married Lady Griffin and that his wife has lost her fortune by marrying without her mother's consent. The climax of the action is the scene in which Deuceace discovers his utter failure and his father's triumphant success. Yellowplush himself had been bribed to change his allegiance at the vital point in the action when he realised the trap into which his master was being drawn. The story closes with a short scene describing the utter destitution of Deuceace and his wife and the amusement which the Earl and Countess of Crabs derive from it when they meet them in the Bois de Boulogne. Yellowplush describes the misery of the young couple and their parents' reaction:

No sooner were my Lord and Lady seated [in their carriage], than they both, with igstream dellixy and good natur, bust into a ror of lafter, peal upon peal, whooping and screaching enough to frighten the evening silents.

DEUCEACE turned round. I see his face now—the face of a devvle of hell! Fust, he lookt towards the carridge, and pinted to it with his maimed arm; then he raised the other, *and struck the woman by his side.* She fell, screaming.

Poor thing! Poor thing!

THE AMOURS OF MR. DEUCEACE III, 337

25

*The Amours of Mr. Deuceace* has considerable power. The Earl of Crabs is the prototype of many of Thackeray's rogues, and in the relationship between him and his son Thackeray succeeded in creating an intense interest. The story has been criticised for presenting a picture of unrelieved and incredible selfishness which it is impossible for the reader to accept; and it must be said that it is difficult to detect a fixed point of reference or a fixed sympathy. The character of Yellowplush undergoes change during the course of the story but it is hard to determine the extent to which he is a hypocritical rogue or a naïve one. Furthermore, it is difficult to reconcile the coolness of the Earl of Crabs and his easy-going selfishness with his behaviour at the end of the story. The final tableau, moreover, is melodramatic, and the way in which Yellowplush presents it is unconvincing. Sometimes Thackeray's use of Yellowplush's point of view allows him to create a startling visual effect, as when he realises the plot and Crabs realises that he has realised the plot. But at other times we feel that the narrator and the characters are playing for effect. This is not objectionable in the Earl, whose character it is to play a part, but it is objectionable when we find that the narrator is manipulating the maimed hand of Deuceace to underline his defeat. The use of the hand is valid in so far as physical maiming is an outward signification of what has happened to Deuceace as a result of his father's superior craft, but it figures too often and in rather too theatrical a manner. When the Earl torments his son by referring to it we can accept it as part of his incredible coolness, but in passages like that at the end of the story and during the discovery scene it becomes a little too obtrusive, acting, as it were, on its own account:

> Deuceace sank down in a chair . . . wriggled madly the stump. . . .
> And here she sank on her knees, and clung to him, and tried to
> catch his hand, and kiss it.
>
> THE AMOURS OF MR. DEUCEACE III, 333 and 335

In maturity Thackeray was frequently to employ a visual effect, and was also to use a kind of theatrical device similar to the one we see here, but in later years both were managed with greater control. In *The Memoirs of Mr. C. J. Yellowplush* devices like these indicate usefully the extent to which Thackeray learned from the theatre, but they do not help to increase the emotional impact of the story.

## 'THE FATAL BOOTS'

Thackeray's next important contribution to a magazine was *The Fatal Boots*, which appeared in George Cruikshank's *Comic Almanack* for 1839. After *The Memoirs of Yellowplush* and before *The Fatal Boots* he published a fantastic burlesque entitled *The Tremendous Adventures of Major Gahagan* (*New Monthly Magazine*, February 1838–February 1839), but *The Fatal Boots* is the first work after *The Memoirs of Yellowplush* in which he can be seen developing his treatment of characteristic themes and subject-matter.

*The Fatal Boots* is an early study of the unconscious rogue, a mean-spirited, selfish and unfeeling bourgeois, convinced of his claim on the attention of society. Nemesis comes to the hero, Bob Stubbs, by means of a childhood attempt to defraud a German bootmaker of a pair of boots. The story, divided into twelve monthly parts and accompanied by illustrations by Cruikshank, relates twelve important incidents in the life of the hero, from a childhood when he was ruined by a foolish mother to a relative destitution which is thoroughly deserved. At each turn in the action Stubbs is pursued by the German bootmaker or by one of the characters uncorrupted by the selfishness of which he is the embodiment.

Stubbs himself controls the stream of incident, relating his own history, and our appreciation of his real character is gained in spite of his unconsciousness of his own meanness and his attempt to pass himself off as a great man. In this respect *The Fatal Boots* shows the influence of Henry Fielding's *Jonathan Wild*, the criminal hero of which is presented throughout as a 'Great Man' who governs his behaviour by a code of selfish materialism. But *The Fatal Boots* lacks consistency and concentration. There is an element of burlesque about the hero, who claims to have been 'eaten by the slugs and harrows of outrageous fortune'. At the beginning of the story Bob Stubbs puts himself forward as a great man, telling us that the adventures we are about to hear '... contain a part of the history of a great, and, confidently I may say, a good man' (III, 541). But after this the element of farce and burlesque becomes too strong for us to take his claim with the small degree of seriousness necessary before an effect or irony can be achieved. It is impossible for the reader to accept Stubbs at his own estimate or to believe in the sincerity of his assertions of goodness or greatness. The ironical method demands that the hero should have a dignity in his own eyes similar to that which Barry Lyndon was to have, or should acquire it from the gaze of a narrator. This condition is not met, and Stubbs's adventures are interesting now only in so far as they are rather amusing and help to explain the development of their creator.

'CATHERINE'

Thackeray's next work has met with little popular success. It was disliked by many readers as it appeared in *Fraser's Magazine* between May 1839 and February 1840, and it was disliked by Thackeray himself. *Catherine* met with some contemporary approbation, but the author found, as the story proceeded, that the subject disgusted him:

> The Judges stand up for me: Carlyle says Catherine is wonderful, and many more laud it highly, but it is a disgusting subject & no mistake. I wish I had taken a pleasanter one & am now and have been for a fortnight in the pains of labour. . . .
>
> Letter to his Mother, 11 February 1840

*Catherine* was a by-product of Thackeray's antagonism to the school of fiction represented by Bulwer Lytton's *Eugene Aram*, Ainsworth's *Jack Shepherd* and Dickens's *Oliver Twist*, the extraordinary success of which caused Thackeray to write his novel. He set out to write a story which would at once reveal the true nature of the criminal type which these and other writers were sentimentalising or glamorising and at the same time sicken the public with an overdose of criminality. He took from the pages of the *Newgate Calendar* the story of Catherine Hayes, burnt alive at

28

Tyburn in 1726 for the brutal murder of her husband. He took every opportunity of pointing out during the course of the story the sordidness and meanness of the characters and their behaviour. And at the end he dismissed his attempt with evident relief and open disgust, saying that the revolting aspects of the tale, its dullness and lowness of tone, all of which critics had pointed out, were calculated effects:

> That [the author] has not altogether failed in the object he had in view, is evident from some newspaper critiques which he has had the good fortune to see; and which abuse the tale of 'Catherine' as one of the dullest, most vulgar, and immoral works extant. It is highly gratifying to the author to find that such opinions are abroad, as they convince him that the taste for Newgate literature is on the wane, and that when the public critic has right down undisguised immorality set before him, the honest creature is shocked at it, as he should be, and can declare his indignation in good round terms of abuse. . . . CATHERINE IV, 669

Besides indicating the extent of Thackeray's objection to sentimental fiction, *Catherine* also shows his preoccupation with a certain type of viciousness. The character who emerges most strongly throughout the course of the narrative is not the heroine herself but the apparently less important Brock or Woods, who changes during the course of years covered by the story from a merely brutal and sly rogue to a figure of greater complexity, the epitome of uninvolved selfishness. While the other characters are drawn into the action by their emotional interests and their selfish concerns, Woods has become by the end of the action almost superhuman, taking pleasure merely in provoking others to evil actions. On the other hand, Catherine herself becomes slightly more human towards the end of the story. Thackeray wrote to his mother when the serialisation was complete:

> . . . it is very ingenious in you to find such beauties in Catherine w$^h$ was a mistake all through—it was not made disgusting enough that is the fact, and the triumph of it would have been to make readers . . . throw up the book and all of its kind, whereas you see the author had a sneaking kindness for his heroine, and did not like to make her utterly worthless. Letter to his Mother, March 1840

As the story develops Catherine's husband, John Hayes, and her illegitimate son eclipse her in selfishness. Catherine shows in her rediscovery of her old lover, the Count de Galgenstein, the emotional susceptibility which, for Thackeray, was to become an increasingly important factor. In contrast to the meanness of Hayes and the swaggering stupidity of her son the capacity of the heroine to become emotionally involved with another person gives her a slight attractiveness which survives the sordidness of the story.

'THE BEDFORD ROW CONSPIRACY'

In one of his frequent letters to his mother Thackeray wrote:

> I find myself growing much more sentimental as I grow older. This world is not near such a bad one as some of your orthodox pretend. We are not desperately wicked but good & loving many of us: our arms reach up to heaven, though the Devil to be sure is tugging at our heels.　　　　　　　Letter to his Mother, 20 August 1840

This was written not long before the sea journey to Ireland during which Isabel Thackeray's insanity became evident, and reflects a mood which was growing in Thackeray during this period, apparently independently of any particular circumstances in his life, and which affected the tone of the work which he produced. In the period between 1840 and 1842 he produced three works in which something like the mature 'embrace of contrasts' or combination of moods became evident. *The Bedford Row Conspiracy* was the first of these.

The basis of the story was a translation of a *nouvelle* by the French novelist Charles de Barnard, called *Le Pied d'Argile*. The satirical elements in the story as Thackeray retells it are very strong, particularly in the case of the hypocritical and self-seeking politician, William Pitt Scully, and his childhood sweetheart, the virtuous but unscrupulous Lady Gorgon. Unlike earlier stories, *The Bedford Row Conspiracy* is told primarily from the point of view, or in the interests, of two characters who are unselfish and ingenuous, the natural victims of the Scullys and the Gorgons. There is also a character who combines wordly wisdom with a basic sympathy for goodness: this is the uncle of the ingenuous hero John Perkins, who condescends to relieve him of his hero-worship for Scully and makes it possible for him to marry the heroine, Lucy Gorgon, niece to the lady who so completely lives up to her name. Without the hero and heroine and our interest in the difficulties of their courtship (difficulties imposed by the selfishness of their connections), *The Bedford Row Conspiracy* would present an unrelieved picture of viciousness such as Thackeray had already achieved in *The Amours of Mr. Deuceace* and *Catherine*. The climax of the story contains a theatrical effect similar to that which closed *The Amours of Mr. Deuceace*, but in this place it is employed for a comic purpose. Scully, completely befooled by Lady Gorgon, is down on his knees before her in John Perkins's apartment. Lady Gorgon has been led to compromise herself with Scully in order to obtain his vote for her husband's party and thus to make sure that he gets a peerage. While this situation is developing the hero and heroine, together with his uncle and her other aunt, Miss Briggs, are approaching the room. They hear the compromisingly intimate pronouncement of Scully's Christian name and enter in time to appreciate the full comedy of the situation between the would-be lover and the elderly flirt.

The comedy of the scene is only in part comedy of situation— it is rendered more complex by the build-up which Thackeray has given to the two people concerned by means of analysis and description of their pretentious dignity, the largeness of their persons and social ambitions. It is also comedy of deflation and reveals the author's increasing ability to manipulate different types of effects, visual, typographical (Lady Gorgon's whimper, 'William,' was in the very smallest print!), and psychological. The final effect is more simply light-hearted than anything which Thackeray attempted later in his career and more subtle than anything which he had previously achieved.

'A SHABBY GENTEEL STORY'

Thackeray seems to have thought that the time when he wrote *A Shabby Genteel Story* was particularly important in his own development. At the end of his life he wrote to his mother:

> Think of the beginning of the story of the little Sister in the Shabby
> Genteel Story twenty years ago and the wife crazy and the Publisher
> refusing me 15 £ who owes me £13.10 and the Times to which I
> apply for a little more than 5 guineas for a week's work, refusing to
> give more and all that money difficulty ended. . . .
>
> Letter to his Mother, 5 July 1862

At the time when he wrote it he intended it to be continued on
the lines which he sketched out in a preface he gave it in 1857—
with Caroline disowned and deserted, 'bitter trials and grief' for
her and a melancholy ending,'—as how should it have been gay?'
Thackeray asked James Fraser, then the editor of the magazine, if
he wanted it to be continued. Apparently the reply was negative
because it was discontinued, to be picked up again in 1862 and
continued as *The Adventures of Philip* when Thackeray wanted a
serial for the *Cornhill Magazine*.

As the title of the story implies, it is concerned with the circumstances of a run-down bourgeois family reduced materially, if
not spiritually, to the device of keeping a boarding house at
Margate and clinging desperately to their 'respectability' and
their past gentility in order to claim the attention of their neigh-
bours. The central character, Caroline Gann, is a Cinderella
figure similar to the heroine of *Miss Shum's Husband* who, like
her, is persecuted by her mother and stepsisters and half-heartedly
protected by a selfish and broken-down father. Like so many of
Thackeray's mothers, Mrs. Gann is a self-righteous, selfish and
cold-hearted woman who inflicts pain and misery on all those
around her who are soft enough to take an impression. Caroline,
undefended by the legacy which each of her stepsisters enjoys, is
her victim and their inferior, overworked, repressed and tor-
mented.

To the lodging-house come two boarders, totally different in
character and social status. The first is a reduced rake, calling
himself Brandon, whose pretensions elevate him above the family
and whose haughtiness offends the two elder sisters (whom he had
hoped to spend the time of his retreat by seducing). After him
comes a Cockney artist, Andrea Fitch, who is in retreat from the
attentions of a fat and wealthy widow who wants to marry him.

Fitch is affectedly Byronic, a preposterous mixture of conceit and earnestness. He becomes more ridiculous when he decides that he has fallen in love with Caroline, but at the same time his 'passion', though affected, is founded on a real emotion and is completely pure. Gradually he wins our respect. On the other hand Brandon, worn out with dissipation and bored in his retreat, makes a callous attempt to seduce Caroline and is frustrated by her innocence and strength of mind. This frustration stimulates a jaded palate to produce a wilful and passionate involvement where Brandon only intended seduction.

As the action develops, Caroline, left exposed to the attentions of the two young men by the selfishness of her family, conceives an affection and admiration for Brandon which is based on the exalted ideas of gentility and sentiment which she has derived from the Gothic and 'silver spoon' novels of the circulating libraries. Inevitably, when it is evident that Caroline favours Brandon and that he has been taking advantage of Andrea in an unfair and supercilious way, the two lovers clash. Brandon treats Andrea with aristocratic scorn; the artist retaliates with a challenge and a duel is arranged. At this point the story begins to speed up and to assume the aspect of situational comedy. Around the lodging-house opposing forces gather, the advent of which Thackeray describes with a touch of the mock heroic. To Brandon come the youthfully decrepit Viscount Cinqbars and the disgusting clerical parasite Tom Tufthunt; to Andrea his elderly adorer Mrs. Carrickfergus and her companion Miss Runt. The climactic scene of the duel ends in farce, but it contains moments of seriousness when Andrea Fitch, facing the fire of Brandon's pistol after his own has been discharged, shows courage and innate dignity of a high order. Brandon returns after the duel demoralised, to be met by Caroline, frantic with news of the duel. Carried away by his own frustrated passion, with the encouragement of the imbecilic Cinqbars and the assistance of Tufthunt, he marries her, without licence or banns, and they leave Margate together.

Throughout this story Thackeray places and relates his characters with consciously dramatic effect and with the clear intention of bringing out those elements in the situation which contribute to his purpose. As the burlesque elements and the occasional incursions into blank verse indicate, the story is concerned with a deliberate balancing and intermingling of emotions. The situation which Thackeray creates is similar to that which he had created in *Miss Shum's Husband*, and the elements of situational comedy are similar to those which he had exploited in *The Amours of Mr. Deuceace* and *The Bedford Row Conspiracy*; but there is a new complexity of motivation and effect in this story. Andrea Fitch has been declared by some critics to be unsatisfactory, and certainly there is a disparity between the method by which he is presented and that used to describe other characters. But this disparity is part of the interest of the story; it contains passages which are clearly by the hand of the creator of Helen Pendennis and Lady Castlewood. The character of Caroline Gann herself is a mixture of foolishness and sincerity, ignorance and purity, more complex than that of earlier heroines like Lucy Gorgon and Mary Shum.

'THE GREAT HOGGARTY DIAMOND'

The history of the Great Hoggarty Diamond is bound up with that of its owner, Samuel Titmarsh, a simple-minded, vain and readily deceived young man, basically honest and good-natured and capable of learning from experience. Samuel Titmarsh's is not the first example of a story told from the point of view of an involved narrator—Bob Stubbs in *The Fatal Boots* told his own story. But Samuel is the first example of a narrator who is writing to explain his own development and is the sentimental hero rather than the rogue.

Titmarsh's gullibility and innocence make him the victim of villains inside and outside his family. He is imposed on by his aunt, whose wealth enables her to live on him, persecuting his wife and forbidding the house to his friend. He is imposed on by his employer, Mr. Brough, chairman of the Independent West Diddlesex Fire and Life Insurance Company, swindler and hypocrite. The list of dramatis personae contains a typical mixture of rogues and innocents, the one a natural prey of the other.

But in Titmarsh's case the very qualities which make him a victim also bring about his salvation, enabling him to make the aristocratic contacts who rescue him from the destitution into which his employer's bankruptcy and the disintegration of the Insurance Company had plunged him. The standards which are important in *The Great Hoggarty Diamond* are those which Thackeray had put forward in earlier work—honesty and good nature and the capacity to feel. The turning point in the fortunes of the Titmarshes comes after the death of their child, when Mary Titmarsh offers herself as a wet nurse to the family whom Samuel had known in the days of his prosperity. Because she yearns for the child she is chosen by the mother instead of another applicant who has every physical qualification but no feeling. A later incident emphasises Samuel's understanding of the cause of his earlier downfall. When Mr. Preston makes improper advances to Mary Titmarsh, is discovered, rejected with laughter and falls into the pond, the good-natured Lord Tiptoff remarks:

> At any rate . . . Titmarsh here has got a place through our friend's unhappy attachment; and Mrs. Titmarsh has only laughed at him, so there is no harm there. It's an ill wind that blows nobody good, you know.　　THE GREAT HOGGARTY DIAMOND III, 113

Titmarsh replies with a somewhat comic dignity which at first gives offence, rejecting the place which Preston had obtained for him:

> Such a wind as that, my Lord, with due respect to you, shall never do good to me. I have learned in the past few years what it is to make friends with the mammon of unrighteousness; and that out of such friendship no good comes in the end to honest men. It shall never be said that Sam Titmarsh got a place because a great man was in love with his wife; and were the situation ten times as valuable, I should blush every day I entered the office-doors in thinking of the base means by which my fortune was made.
> 　　　　　THE GREAT HOGGARTY DIAMOND III, 113

At the end of the story Sam is still honest, good-natured and sentimental, but he has grown up and realised that it was not innocence alone which allowed him to be fooled, but cupidity. Samuel is the first of the innocent characters who learn how to defend themselves in a world of rogues by clinging to the standards which make them vulnerable. Like his mother and sisters, who remain poor and happy in Somerset, Samuel Titmarsh learns that happiness is not to be gained and kept by means of a diamond pin or a place in an Insurance Office—but he also learns that honesty in action is not enough without an honest analysis of one's own motivation.

### 'FITZ-BOODLE'S CONFESSIONS'

In George Fitz-Boodle, Esquire, whose confessions began to appear in *Fraser's Magazine* in June 1842, Thackeray created a unique type of narrator, a 'heavy' young man of aristocratic birth and classical education. Fitz-Boodle begins as a self-revelatory character, exposing his own faults and limitations, unaware that they are anything but virtues; he is arrogant in his scorn for the literary profession, and his sole criterion is knowledge of the ways of the polite world. Gradually, however, Fitz-Boodle begins to lose these characteristics and to become broader in his interests, more sensitive and humane, until he develops into the narrator of *Men's Wives*.

### 'MEN'S WIVES'

As the narrator of the series of stories which Thackeray published in *Fraser's Magazine* under this title (between March and October 1843) Fitz-Boodle is less prominent as a character but entirely sympathetic. Of the three stories (there were originally four, but one was left out when the series was published in book form) one, *Mr. and Mrs. Frank Berry*, centres around a personal relationship which began at school: another, *Dennis Haggarty's Wife*, is built on a framework of several meetings between the narrator and the hero: but the third and longest, *The Ravenswing*, has only very slight connections with the narrator's life. Fitz-Boodle is not important as a narrator in the same way as Samuel Titmarsh, or even Yellowplush.

This does not mean that *Men's Wives* does not have unity of tone or purpose. In these three stories Thackeray substantially developed his interest in the area of experience which was to figure prominently in *The Newcomes*. All three stories centre on marital relationships involving selfishness and callousness on one side and dependent affection on the other. *The Ravenswing* also deals with relationships outside marriage.

The heroine after whom this story is named is Morgiana Crump, daughter of a retired dancer and a footman who keep a public house under the name of The Bootjack. Morgiana only gains the name of the Ravenswing when she has taken to the stage herself. At The Bootjack she is courted by two gentlemen, Archibald Eglantine, a hairdresser, and Mr. Woolsey, junior partner in a firm of tailors. Each of the gentlemen suffers under a personal disadvantage; as Fitz-Boodle says:

> Now, it was a curious fact, that these two gentlemen were each in need of the other's services—Woolsey being afflicted with premature baldness, or some other necessity for a wig still more fatal—Eglantine being a very fat man, who required much art to make his figure at all decent.　　　　　　　　　THE RAVENSWING IV, 370

In a permanent state of rivalry for the hand of Morgiana, Woolsey and Eglantine are galvanised into co-operation by the arrival of a third and dangerous suitor—Captain Howard Walker, a swindling rake and man-about-town with unsubstantial military rank, dyed moustaches and a gentlemanly air. They agree to help each other, and in due course Mr. Eglantine gives Mr. Woolsey a perfect wig and Mr. Woolsey returns the compliment with a coat which turns fatness to dignity. Unfortunately for both of them, Walker, spurred on by the delusion that Morgiana's dowry amounts to £5,000 rather than £500, succeeds in dis-uniting them and making them look ridiculous, carrying off the impressionable Morgiana himself.

The married life of Morgiana and Walker is not a happy one, though things go well enough until a chance incident springs the mine of bankruptcy under Walker's feet. His wife does every-thing she can to save him, though her innocence actually makes the situation worse, and with a brutality which he had previously had no opportunity of showing, Walker blames her, beats her, and makes her go to her former lovers with requests for assistance.

The original cause of the financial crisis which sends Walker to the Fleet was a bill for the singing lessons which Morgiana had been receiving from the amorous Benjamin Barowski, a Jewish impresario whose clumsy attempts at seduction she had repelled with healthy violence. After her husband's imprisonment and the birth of her child Morgiana takes to the stage under the tutelage of Sir George Thrum, Barowski's rival, supported and encouraged by the faithful Woolsey. From his prison Walker continues the exploitation of his wife, using his power over her to force her managers to compound for his debts and obtain his release. Once out of prison he continues his unfeeling brutality, adding blatant infidelity to the list of his misdeeds and making Morgiana support with the proceeds of her singing a mistress and 'a great number of over-dressed children'.

At this point the story ends, but a footnote in the form of a letter from Fitz-Boodle to Oliver Yorke, the pseudonymous editor of *Fraser's*, informs us that Walker has drunk himself to death in America and that Morgiana is now married to Mr. Woolsey.

The footnote, however, is no more than a footnote, and the dominant tone of the story is not in harmony with the happy ending. There is nothing tragic about *The Ravenswing* though, even without the footnote, because the heroine's capacity for feeling is limited by an essentially robust and rather vulgar constitution. Morgiana is not a creature from the same mould as Caroline Gann or Amelia of *Vanity Fair*; she is, like Woolsey, a 'good' character, because of her capacity to give and to receive affection, but the range and duration of her emotions are limited. Even in the days of her misfortune Morgiana shows something of the capacity for self-deceit which Thackeray was later to depict so strikingly in both the vicious and virtuous. And the concern for her feelings which Woolsey expresses in the footnote implies that he too is capable of allowing affection to dull his perception:

> I knew you, Mr. Fitz-Boodle, at once, but did not mention your name for fear of agitating my wife.     THE RAVENSWING IV, 475

*The Ravenswing* is the longest and the fullest of the three stories grouped under the title of *Men's Wives. Mr. and Mrs. Frank Berry* is a striking portrayal of a character in the process of disintegration under the domination of a small-minded, self-centred wife. The third story, *Dennis Haggarty's Wife*, tells a miserable story of the capture of a naïve and good-natured Irish army surgeon by a husband-hunting mother and daughter. The story falls into three parts concerned with three meetings between Fitz-Boodle and Haggarty: the first at Leamington, where Haggarty proposes for Julia Gam and is rejected; the second in Ireland, where Fitz-Boodle learns of the subsequent marriage of Dennis and Julia; the third at Richmond, where Fitz-Boodle learns from the heart-broken Haggarty the miserable sequel and the story of his desertion and exploitation by his selfish wife and vicious mother-in-law.

All three stories show Thackeray's developing sensitivity to human relationships and to the implications of character. At several points the narrative rises to the level of the later work, showing something of Thackeray's ability to generalise on a particular situation, relating an individual trait to a human law. Such a point is reached when Fitz-Boodle allows his imagination to wander into the upper regions of the stately and dingy mansion of Sir George Thrum:

> There is something awful in the bedroom of a respectable old couple of sixty-five. Think of the old feathers, turbans, bugles, petticoats, pomatum-pots, spencers, white satin shoes, false fronts, the old flaccid boneless stays tied up in faded riband, the dusky fans, the old forty-years-old baby linen, the letters of Sir George when he was young, the doll of poor Maria who died in 1803, Frederick's first corduroy breeches, and the newspaper which contains the account of his distinguishing himself at the siege of Seringapatam. All these lie somewhere, damp and squeezed down into glum old presses and wardrobes. At that glass the wife has sat many times these fifty years; in that old morocco bed her children were born. Where are they now? THE RAVENSWING IV, 450–1

This passage is indicative of the mature talent which was so soon to develop, but other parts of *Men's Wives* show that Thackeray had reached a degree of bitterness which he was never to exceed and was prepared to make statements of a satiric directness which is unusual anywhere in his work. In *Dennis Haggarty's Wife* Thackeray, by means of Fitz-Boodle, commits himself to a statement of central importance to his position as a satirist. Fitz-Boodle says:

> There is a quality in certain people which is above all advice, exposure, or correction. Only let a man or woman have DULNESS sufficient, and they need bow to no extant authority. A dullard recognises no betters; a dullard can't see that he is in the wrong; a dullard has no scruples of conscience, no doubts of pleasing, or succeeding . . . no respect but for the fool himself. How can you make a fool perceive he is a fool? Such a personage can no more see his own folly than he can see his own ears. And the great quality of Dulness is to be unalterably contented with itself.
>
> DENNIS HAGGARTY'S WIFE IV, 505

At the end of the story, moved by the unspeakable viciousness of the self-righteous women who ruined Dennis Haggarty, Fitz-Boodle directs a powerful and moving tirade against them and the story ends on a note of sustained bitterness more direct than anything else Thackeray wrote. In his later work the statement which Fitz-Boodle makes is often present but it is always qualified or balanced by means of another. *Men's Wives* is the most consistently satirical of his works. It reflects a mood which was not to recur but out of which all his later work was to develop.

'BARRY LYNDON'

After *Men's Wives* Thackeray produced his last important contribution to *Fraser's Magazine* and his most substantial story before *Vanity Fair—The Memoirs of Barry Lyndon Esq. written by himself,* which appeared in the magazine from January to September and in November and December 1844. The idea for the story came to him in the summer of 1841, when he first learnt the story of the adventurer, Andrew Robinson Stoney, whose career formed the basis of the later part of *Barry Lyndon*. The hero of Thackeray's story is a rogue, brutal, vicious and self-deceived, and Thackeray's intention in writing it was partly to make a striking demonstration of the self-righteousness of the morally insensitive such as he had already commented on in *Men's Wives*. He also attempted to delineate the moral disintegration of a character at first possessed of some not unadmirable qualities, showing in the progress of this character from youth to age the brutalising effects of the standards by which he had lived and of the success which his swaggering energies had brought him. At the same time he was interested (and this reflects the later interest which produced *The History of Henry Esmond* and *The Virginians*) in analysing the social changes which had come about during the half-century which separated Lyndon's generation from his own, approving by implication the increase in social restraint and the development of a new and milder concept of gentility which he himself did much to forward.

Because he had more than one purpose in writing the story, *Barry Lyndon* is more complex in structure and effect than the work on which (in this and this alone like *The Fatal Boots*) it is modelled—Fielding's *Jonathan Wild*. In order to achieve his basic aim and make the rogue expose himself, Thackeray had to ensure that Barry's account of himself contained facts which were not compatible with his own opinion. Barry had to be made to reveal his real quality without realising it himself, and the reader had to be made aware of the need to exercise his own judgment at Barry's expense. On the whole this is brilliantly achieved but there are times when Thackeray wanted to use Barry's experiences in order to make a point about human behaviour or social structure. Barry's account of his service with the army of Frederick the Great during the Seven Years' War reflects Thackeray's personal convictions about warfare, politics and immediate European history. When Barry is telling us about the brutality in Frederick's army there is no disparity between his judgment of the situation and ours. Similarly, when he is discussing the causes of Irish poverty or describing the state of the streets in 18th-century Dublin Barry is the representative of his creator's opinions. After such passages of agreement it is difficult for the reader to adjust himself to the presence of irony and to remember that he must keep his distance from the hero in order to make a proper assessment of his moral status.

Certain incidents in the story are also difficult to reconcile with a consistent purpose in the author. The episode at the Court of the Duke of X—— is an important part of Barry's history in that it shows him as an aggressor for the first time and reveals the extent to which he is morally degraded, so that he can attempt to achieve a vile purpose by the viler means of blackmail. Barry has acted wildly before he attempts to win the Countess Ida but his doing so has always been partially excusable by circumstances and the energy and resourcefulness with which he endured and avoided authorised brutality. At the Court Barry has no stimulus to act except his own desire for gain and no sensitivity towards the terrible issues involved in the game which he is playing. Here, in the violence with which certain of the characters react to him, we first begin to see Barry from the outside. The earlier extension of vision which we received in the reported conversation of the Prussian Chief of Police and Barry's Captain prepared the ground for our eventual acceptance of a hostile assessment of the adventurer, but we were unable to accept it at the time because of the evident bias of the people involved in it. Against the refinement of the courtiers and the moral sensitivity of characters like Baron Magny and the young Duke, Barry begins to appear in a poorer light than he is aware of.

The incident of the intrigue between the younger Magny and the Princess also makes clear the full extent of Barry's insensitivity and his willingness to trade on human misery. But this end is achieved in the narration of Barry himself and the continuation of the story by Madame de Liliengarten adds nothing to our understanding of his character. The explanation of the circumstances which lay behind the arrest of Magny and which caused the expulsion of Barry and his uncle from the ducal territory is a reflection of Thackeray's interest in the general matter of the transformation of social behaviour which took place between the later 18th century and the early 19th, the period from which his own generation sprang. Madame de Liliengarten's narration is a striking comment on the social situation in which Barry could be so nearly successful and in which the lack of restraint other than that imposed by the laws of superficial politeness would bring terrible consequences. It is significant that the end of Barry's stay in X—— should be brought about by the young Duke, who also, when he comes to power, recalls the troops which have been sold to foreign powers and puts an end to public gambling. The succession of the new Duke marks the beginning of the period in which Barry is out of place, in which he can find a home only in the debtor's prison.

Social history and the character of the rogue are thus closely related, though the relation is not direct. A third interest which Thackeray had was more difficult to relate to the central matter of the rogue's self-revelation. Thackeray wanted to show us a 'hero' in the novel writer's sense of the word exposing himself for what he really was—a man of action at the expense of every human feeling. At the same time he wished to show us the process by which an idealistic, affectionate and attractively brave boy became a brutal, cowardly drunkard. Because his primary purpose led him to make Barry his own narrator it conflicted with his secondary purpose, in that it made it difficult for him to show the process of change. The difficulty arose over the way in which he was to make an old reprobate, completely insensitive to any code higher than that of the duel, describe himself as a relatively pure and sensitive child without himself being aware of the disintegration. Thackeray overcame this difficulty by making Barry aware of his own decline and attribute it to factors which we can see are only partially responsible for it, if at all. Thus he blames his ultimate decline in fortune on bad luck, while he is unwilling to attribute his previous success to anything other than his own qualities; he blames his physical decline, while we can see the gradual changes in the world around him which have made his violence an element which can no longer operate within the pattern of social activity. Barry is able to see the change in himself and the world around him only in a limited and distorted way. We have our eyes opened by his monstrous complacency and are aware of the same changes in wider moral and social perspective.

Thackeray was interested in these social changes primarily because he saw the assertion of the rule of law as being ultimately interdependent with the rule of feeling which binds one human being to another. Barry begins as a person who is able to feel— his calf-love for his cousin Norah Brady is foolish, but shows him erring on the side of innocence rather than that of the worldly experience which Thackeray often thought of in close association with the idea of guilt. What changes and eventually ruins Barry is the combination of ideas which he had assimilated from his mother during childhood: that he was a gentleman; that being such entitled him to demand a fine living from society; and that his own person and the cultivation of it were the legitimate and even the highest ends at which he could aim; that the only code by which he should govern himself was that of honour. This collection of ideas gets him a long way but the central irony of the story is that it leads ultimately to the Fleet by a natural process. Barry, in a rare moment of truth, points out that he was made to make rather than to keep a fortune. When he has succeeded in marrying Lady Lyndon, with her income of £40,000 a year, he has reached the highest point available to him. From then on the force of his own momentum and the violence of his energy and activity is rendered purposeless and self-destructive. He is a man who has only one idea of purposeful activity—the betterment of his own material conditions. This comes over most vividly in his scorn for men of letters and his failure to see that what they could offer him could save him from himself.

Thackeray manipulates the reader's awareness of the values involved in Barry's career and of the principles against which he offends partly by exploiting the hero's own dullness. He makes Barry report remarks and situations which are to his own discredit, though he cannot see it himself. The remark of George III about Barry's American company is an example of this device:

> 'That's right, Mr. Lyndon, raise another company: and go with them too!'  BARRY LYNDON IV, 228

Thackeray also permits Barry's editing of his own experiences occasionally to break down, so that information, which the narrator has attempted to keep back, filters through to the reader. By the time that Barry courts Lady Lyndon, after her husband's death, we are quite well acquainted with his character, but we are still prepared to allow him the full measure of physical beauty which he claims for himself. A chance remark of Viscount Bullingdon's warns us to take more care. When Lady Lyndon pretends to Lord George Poynings that she does not know Barry Lyndon her child remarks:

> 'Oh yes, mamma,' . . . 'the tall dark man at Spa with the cast in his eye, who used to make my governor tipsy and sent me the sword; his name is Mr. Barry.'                               IV, 187

A similar effect is created by the derogatory remarks of Sir Charles Lyndon, whose aspersions on his birth and breeding Barry is too stupidly proud to hold back, and by the various glimpses which we catch of the stream of mistresses he had after his marriage.

What most surely damns Barry Lyndon, however, is not our assessment of his birth, his breeding or his appearance. Even when these factors are taken into consideration he remains an interesting and exciting character. If he has swagger rather than gentility (as his uncle points out), and if he is lacking in the higher qualities of imagination, self-control, education, yet he still has the lower quality of energy in abundance. What prevents us from keeping a qualified respect for him is the way in which other characters learn to withdraw from him and to understand that his influence and presence are pernicious. Among such characters are Countess Ida and Viscount Bullingdon, the Rector of Hackton and Redmond Quin, as well as the foolish but pathetic Lady Lyndon. Through their revulsion we learn the full extent of Barry's degradation and depravity.

Powerful though *Barry Lyndon* is, Thackeray was not pleased with it. The story did not appeal to the public, who objected to the presentation of immorality, regardless of the purpose behind it, and who were incapable of realising that it was ironical. Thackeray tired of it in much the same way as he tired of *Catherine*, and found increasing difficulty in writing it, failing altogether to produce an instalment in time for October 1844; and he strongly expressed his relief when he eventually finished it. His dislike is partly explicable in terms of the structure of the story, the main movement being one of disintegration. The change in tone from the beginning to the end is a dismal one, the shift in the sympathy which is required of the reader being almost strong enough to make him protest his early attraction for the hero against the unrelieved picture of misery which the ageing Lyndon creates around himself.

Yet *Barry Lyndon*, in spite of its gloom and the slight structural weakness caused by Thackeray's multiple purpose, is the most powerful work which he created up to 1844. Of all the stories which he had written since 1836 it is the most nearly successful, and taken together with *Men's Wives* it shows many of the attitudes which were involved in his later novels. *Barry Lyndon* marks the point at which Thackeray stood at the end of his apprenticeship; it grew out of an attempt to achieve something of the popular success which was being achieved by Dickens, Harrison Ainsworth and Charles Lever, whose *Harry Lorrequer* was in his mind when he began it; and it was almost his last unsuccessful attempt on the mass reading public. By 1844 he was one of the best known and most successful magazine writers but had still not attracted the attention of the larger public. In the early years the reason for this was the immaturity of his work —*The Memoirs of Yellowplush*, and *The Fatal Boots* did not deserve more widespread popularity than they received. But in the work which he produced in 1843–4 there were no signs of immaturity, though it suffered from a narrowness of appeal and showed a severity of tone which did not attract the soft-hearted Victorian public. Yet even at its best this work is deficient when judged by the standards of *Vanity Fair*; it lacks something of that elusive complexity of tone and depth of perception into human situations that we associate with him at his best. During the seven years from *Yellowplush* to *Barry Lyndon* Thackeray had developed greatly, but his development was not complete. Over the next three years the process was brought to completion: his life changed, his character changed, he found a subject and wrote *Vanity Fair*.

# 3

# Defining his Terms

*Barry Lyndon* was finished while Thackeray was in quarantine at Malta in October 1846, after a voyage round the Middle East which formed the basis of his sketch book, *Notes of a Journey from Cornhill to Cairo.* This was the third of the sketch books which Thackeray published as independent volumes. The first of of them was the *Paris Sketch Book* (1840), which consisted of a loosely connected series of tales, essays and reports on the contemporary situation at Paris, many of which had been separately published before collection in book form. The second was the *Irish Sketch Book* (1843), which Thackeray had conceived as a more unified work than its predecessor and for which he was contracted with Chapman and Hall as early as September 1840. The opportunity for the voyage to the Middle East came at short notice, one night in August 1844. A chance invitation of a free passage gave Thackeray only three days' notice before he set off. *Notes of a Journey from Cornhill to Cairo* records the impressions he received; it was published in January 1846.

These three books were important to Thackeray because they were his only attempts before *Vanity Fair* to capture the imagination of the book-reading public with original material. To a certain extent they succeeded in doing this and his increasing reputation during the early forties is reflected in the growing sales of the successive sketch books and the increasing interest of publishers in his work.

The three sketch books, written over a period of six years, also show the development of Thackeray's characteristic attitudes during the most eventful and trying period of his life. All three works were attacked by contemporary reviewers and have since been criticised for superficiality. But it is this quality that makes them valuable to the student of Thackeray. In writing them he was very conscious of the need for doing something which had not been done before by any of the authors who had attempted to introduce insular English readers to Europe, Asia or Ireland. He takes pains to point out that he is writing from an individual point of view, and particularly from that of a Cockney, or urbanised Englishman of the middle classes. The danger of this attitude is shown often enough in the *Irish Sketch Book*, where the transference of English attitudes to Irish subjects gives the impression of narrow-mindedness and smugness, but on the other hand it also produces the peculiar interest of many parts of that work where Thackeray gives close attention to a point of Irish culture or Irish society which has attracted his interest.

Of the three books, *Notes of a Journey from Cornhill to Cairo* probably comes nearest to complete success. The *Paris Sketch Book* contains many tales which are of some interest, but on the whole the book is immature, revealing a mixture of sentiment and prejudice and more insular smugness than the other volumes. The *Irish Sketch Book* is more free from this spirit but the very subject—of intense interest in England during the middle years of the century—meant that Thackeray was under constant pressure to judge Irish events and society by standards which were foreign to it. On the whole the best parts of the book are those where Thackeray discusses the literature of the people and makes game out of his own role of tourist. *Notes of a Journey from Cornhill to Cairo* took Thackeray a long way from England and farther from English prejudices than the other two works. Perhaps because of this factor, and the fact that he was older when he wrote it, the book shows a freer play of fantasy and a more acceptable operation of the moralistic tendency.

Before he wrote *Notes of a Journey . . .* , and even before he finished *Barry Lyndon*, Thackeray had begun writing for *Punch*, which was during the next few years to be an increasing source of income and of reputation to him. It is not known when he became a contributor for the first time, but his first large-scale contribution was *Miss Tickletoby's Lectures on English History* which appeared in the magazine between July and October 1842 and were discontinued because they were not popular.

THACKERAY AND 'PUNCH'

*Punch* was founded in 1841 as a result of the efforts of Mark Lemon and Henry Mayhew. Its first few months were difficult ones, partly because the public associated it with other humorous papers which traded on indecency and scandal. The history of *Punch*'s early years is the history of an outcast becoming a member of the Establishment. At first Radical, irresponsibly satirical and light-hearted, *Punch* grew to respect the institutions of Britain and to assume patriotic, middle-class and eventually jingoistic airs. To some extent the changes which took place in its early years were the result of the influence of Thackeray himself and other contributors who felt as he did. The change which the magazine underwent was matched by a change which took place in Thackeray, as he acquired popularity and came to feel the responsibility which it brought. In part both changes were a manifestation of a wider change which was coming about in society as a whole; or they were merely part of the inevitable process through which Englishmen and English institutions go. *Punch* followed *Blackwood's Magazine*, *Fraser's* and even the *Quarterly Review* in leaving behind early light-heartedness and irresponsibility and taking on a mood of increased steadiness and respectability as it grew older.

Before and after the failure of *Miss Tickletoby's Lectures* Thackeray contributed many minor pieces of humour, satire and comment. H. S. Gulliver, in his study of Thackeray's early writings, estimates the number of his contributions during 1844 and 1845 at one hundred and fifty and gives a list of thirty pseudonyms under which he wrote. But Thackeray's major contributions did not appear until after he had been accepted as a regular member of the staff who drew a monthly salary and attended the weekly dinners at which editorial policy was discussed. This occurred some time in 1844. In the same year appeared a series of papers under the pseudonym of 'The Fat Contributor', in whom he created one of his popular narrators. One of the most notable

DT                                                                    49 propensities of this personage was pointed out in a supposedly editorial note to the 'Love Song of the Fat Contributor':

> When he went abroad last—to join General Taylor in Mexico—the F.C. left us with a bundle of MSS., on various scraps of paper, and in different stages of his handwriting. They were tied up with an old piece of ribbon and entitled 'Passion Flowers'; they are signed Frederick Chumleigh, Ferdinand Cavendish, Frank Chesterfield, Fulke Cadogan, Fitzroy Clarence (all names with the initials F. C., which in fact are his own, and which led us humorously to call him the Fat Contributor).

Quoted from H. S. Gulliver, THACKERAY'S LITERARY APPRENTICESHIP 157

The Fat Contributor is driven by an irresistible desire to make fantasies about himself and reacts with timorous alacrity to the stimulus provided by beauty or sublimity. The comedy of his many situations springs from the mingling of his vanity and vapourings with an honesty of reaction and report about himself, and results in a pleasing combination of the affecting and the humorous.

The adventures of the F. C. are closely connected with those of Thackeray himself because both of them gave an account of their travels in the Middle East and Mediterranean and the same material is used in both accounts. Comparison of these two records shows the ease with which Thackeray could manipulate a *persona* and indicates the care with which he qualified the Fat Contributor's vanity with his good feeling and made comic the disparity between his ideal picture of the world and the reality which his adventures forced on his attention, making this the source of comedy rather than the satire which a similar disparity had occasioned in the case of characters who did not possess the Fat Contributor's softer qualities. The F. C. is a pleasant character because he can feel for others in a genuine way, though his feelings are affected and comic, and he is saved by a humility and honesty in the face of experience which all Thackeray's 'good' characters at one time or another show.

'THE BOOK OF SNOBS'

The papers of the Fat Contributor were in part a rest from more serious labours and an excursion in a more light-hearted mood than was frequent with Thackeray during these years. In *Punch* at the same time there appeared other contributions which were primarily humorous rather than satirical. Yellowplush was revived with a more attractive character in *Jeames's Diary*, which ridiculed the railway mania of the 1840s. But it was only with the beginning of the series of Snob papers which ran in *Punch* from February 1846 to February 1847 that Thackeray made his first break-through into the kind of popularity which had been enjoyed already for some years by Dickens and Lever. The success was justified because in these papers Thackeray wrote for the first time with consistent ability, leaving behind many of the faults of the earlier writing, and with breadth of appeal. *The Book of Snobs* is not a novel and has something of the narrowness of range which belongs to a social document. Although it is a great deal more than the demonstration of a thesis, it contains a clear exposition of Thackeray's social statement and had a considerable influence on contemporary thought about society and social behaviour.

The idea of the Snob as it appears in this work was the result of Thackeray's own expansion of the word contained in the title of the undergraduate publication with which he had been connected. In early Victorian England the snob was a member of the lower middle, trading or commercial classes who had some pretensions to gentility or consideration. A snob was a newcomer or a social outsider, and the word is frequently used to imply no more than that, both before and after Thackeray had taken it up and changed its meaning. He took up the associations of the word with the brasher and more pretentious aspects of middle-class behaviour, and extended it in this direction so as to include not merely the attempt to ape one's betters but also the attempt to base a claim for attention on social position or superficial considerations of breeding or financial status. He made it a concept which included the Prince Regent and Beau Brummel and anyone else (irrespective of their position in the old social hierarchy) who showed in his bearing towards others that he valued superficial considerations above others. In doing this he also altered the meaning of the word 'gentleman', of which the Prince Regent and Brummel had previously been the most outstanding examples, so as to exclude them and to include only those who showed in their conduct and bearing towards others true moral perspective and sensitivity. His attack was directed against snobbery not merely in external observances and social life but in marital and familial relationships, in treatment of inferiors and superiors and in the estimation of oneself.

One of the most marked features of *The Book of Snobs* is the character of the narrator, who freely admits to being one of the body himself but who maintains his objective vision and perspective. Mr. Snob is the first example in Thackeray's work of the omniscient narrator who is engaged in the events which he is describing and in the social milieu which he is attacking and who, at the same time, has a relationship with the reader outside the context of his actual narration. The result of this is a peculiar complexity of effect. Thackeray ranges from straightforward satire, such as that which he directs against the Prince Regent and the Royal Flunkeys, to intimacy and involvement. A snob, he says, is 'He who meanly admires mean things. . . .' Into this category fall characters like the City Snob, Mr. Pump, whose admiration for the rank of an aristocratic wife makes him find an enquiry after her health over-familiar:

> Mr. Pump looked exceedingly puzzled and disgusted, and after a pause, said, '*Lady Blanche Pump* is pretty well, I thank you.'
>
> THE BOOK OF SNOBS VI, 332

It also includes figures like that of Lieutenant-General the Honourable Sir George Granby Tufto, K.C.B., K.T.S., K.H., K.S.W., &c. &c. whose treatment is as savage as that which Thackeray earlier gave to Dennis Haggarty's wife and mother-in-law:

> A man can't help being a fool, be he ever so old, and Sir George is a greater ass at sixty-eight than he was when he first entered the army at fifteen. . . . It is difficult to say what virtues this prosperous gentleman possesses. He never read a book in his life, and, with his purple, old gouty fingers, still writes a schoolboy hand. He has reached old age and grey hairs without being the least venerable. . . . On account

of his rank and his services, people pay the bestarred and betitled old
brute a sort of reverence; and he looks down upon you and me, and
exhibits his contempt for us, with a stupid and artless candour which
is quite amusing to watch.                                    VI, 335-6

Brilliant as this portrait is, however, it shows a kind of brilliance which Thackeray had achieved before when he was concerned with an individual whose outlook on the world was
totally distorted by self-complacency. What is new in *The Book
of Snobs* is that such portraits are part of a consistent and penetrating presentation of that wide area of life in which social behaviour
and moral values come into conflict, and also part of a context in
which each shade of portraiture and category of treatment is
manipulated with striking effect.

An important part of this effect is created by the personality of
the narrator, Mr. Snob. He is not consistent as a personality,
shifting with the author's intention, emerging more openly at
some times than at others, taking more or less responsibility for
the social evils which he describes. But he is consistent in admitting the application of his own satire to himself and in qualifying
his penetrating criticism of individuals and types by strongly
expressed admiration of the qualities which are opposed to those
which he is attacking. He is demonstrably no cynic, and if he
attacks selfishness and stupidity when he sees them embodied in
characters like Mrs. Ponto, and the products of servility and
flattery like Sir George Tufto, he also has a keen sensibility which
allows him to appreciate the complexity of the situation in which
characters like Major Ponto find themselves. In the papers concerned with Country Snobs, and in that which tells the sad tale of
Mr. Sackville the coal merchant, he shows his understanding of
the fine distinction between those who are the victims of endemic
snobbism and those who are beyond the reach of finer feelings.
Ponto, trapped by his own admiration for the false principle
dominant in the society around him, becomes a victim to his son's
extravagance without being able to see the remedy or even to
detect a fault. The apparently harmless snobbism of Ponto has
such severe repercussions as to enable us to see him as the victim

of a force more powerful than himself. His reaction to his son's bill is pathetic:

> 'Lord Gules tells me he is the most careful youngster in the regiment, God bless him! But look at that! by Heaven, Snob, look at that and say how can a man of nine hundred keep out of the Bench?' He gave a sob as he handed me the paper across the table; and his old face, and his old corduroys, and his shrunk shooting-jacket, and his lean shanks looked, as he spoke, more miserably haggard, bankrupt, and threadbare.
> VI, 405

Thackeray wrote at the end of *The Book of Snobs*:

> You who despise your neighbour, are a Snob; you who forget your own friends, meanly to follow after those of a higher degree, are a Snob; you who are ashamed of your poverty, and blush for your calling, are a Snob; as are you who boast of your pedigree, or are proud of your wealth.
>
> To laugh at such is *Mr. Punch's* business. May he laugh honestly, hit no foul blow, and tell the truth when at his very broadest grin—never forgetting that if Fun is good, Truth is still better, and Love best of all.
> VI, 464

When he had written this he wrote to the editor of *Punch*, Mark Lemon, saying:

> That concluding benedictory paragraph in the Snobs I hope won't be construed in any unpleasant way by any other labourer on the paper. I mean of course I hope Jerrold won't fancy that I reflect on him now as he did in the Parson-Snob Controversy. I think his opinions are wrong on many points, but I am sure he believes them honestly, and I don't think that he or any man *has* hit a foul blow in Punch.
>
> What I mean applies to my own case & that of all of us—who set up as Satirical-Moralists—and having such a vast multitude of readers whom we not only amuse but teach. And indeed, a solemn prayer to God Almighty was in my thoughts that we may never forget truth & Justice and kindness as the great end of our profession. There's something of the same strain in Vanity Fair. A few years ago I should have sneered at the idea of setting up as a teacher at all, and perhaps at this pompous and pious way of talking about a few papers of jokes in Punch—but I have got to believe in the business, and in

many other things since then. And our profession seems to me to be as serious as the Parson's own. Please God we'll be honest & kind was what I meant and all I meant. I swear nothing more.

Letter to Mark Lemon, 24 February 1847

This letter was necessary because of a controversy which had sprung up between Thackeray and Douglas Jerrold, his rival for popularity among readers of *Punch*, and a man with whom he came increasingly to disagree during the course of their association on its staff. Jerrold was a radical—so at one time was Thackeray—and they were both satirists, attacking much the same objects. But Jerrold stood with Dickens in thinking that the salvation of Victorian England depended on direct political and social reform which could be brought about by the kind of satire which the latter directed at the Circumlocution Office in *Little Dorrit*. Thackeray, on the other hand, was coming more and more to investigate the relationship between social behaviour and moral standards and to believe that satire should be qualified by sentiment and directed not towards institutions but towards certain tendencies in human nature. Although he had quarrelled with his mother over religion and refused to accept her brand of Evangelicalism, he came more and more in his later years to associate social reform with the application of principles of 'truth, Justice and kindness', and more and more to take a passive part in political debate.

Once Thackeray began to feel like this—and the letter which he wrote to Lemon indicates the process by which he did so—active collaboration with Radicals like Jerrold and Dickens was impossible. It was over their writing for *Punch*, which had originally brought them together, that the disagreement between Jerrold and Thackeray grew into antagonism. The first clash between them came over Jerrold's antipathy towards the clergy and culminated in a quarrel over Chapter 11 of *The Book of Snobs*. Eventually the widening gap led Thackeray to dissociate himself from the magazine and to resign from the staff in 1851.

To a certain extent this last act was the result of a change in Thackeray himself as well as of his clash with other people involved in the magazine. By the time he finished *The Book of Snobs* he had already published two numbers of *Vanity Fair* and written a third. Before long the novel caught on, and Thackeray had the rewards as well as the responsibilities of a vast popular audience. Between 1848 and 1863 he made a great deal of money and was able to stand on his own feet, independent of magazine writing for an income and unaffected to a greater extent than Dickens by the comments of his critics or by a sense that he should be developing his mode of writing. Thackeray worked a long time for popularity and took it easily when it came, wisely exploiting his reputation as a writer to make money as a lecturer and free himself from the necessity of writing for a living. By the time that he wrote *The Book of Snobs*, Thackeray was fully mature and confident in his own attitude as a writer, with a clear sense of purpose and a determination to attempt the serious task which he had set himself. Of this new maturity and confidence *Vanity Fair* was the first result.

# 4

# 'Vanity Fair'

Thackeray began to publish *Vanity Fair* in January 1847, but it was conceived and partly written long before. What evidence there is about its conception indicates that although it may have been in his mind for some years it was not actually begun until some time in 1844. By May 1845 it had been refused by Colburn, who, according to Thackeray's biographer, Gordon Ray, was the third or fourth publisher to whom the manuscript was submitted. At this stage the novel consisted only of a draft of Chapters 1–4 and 6. It seems to have been accepted by Bradbury and Evans by January 1846 and planned for publication from May of that year, although various delays and revisions meant that publication was held up until the following January. Then the novel appeared in regular monthly numbers containing three or four chapters until the last double number in July 1848. The relationship between chapters and numbers was as follows:

| | |
|---|---|
| I, Chapters 1–4 | X, Chapters 33–5 |
| II, Chapters 5–7 | XI, Chapters 36–8 |
| III, Chapters 8–11 | XII, Chapters 39–42 |
| IV, Chapters 12–14 | XIII, Chapters 43–6 |
| V, Chapters 15–18 | XIV, Chapters 47–51 |
| VI, Chapters 19–22 | XV, Chapters 51–3 |
| VII, Chapters 23–5 | XVI, Chapters 54–6 |
| VIII, Chapters 26–9 | XVII, Chapters 57–60 |
| IX, Chapters 30–2 | XVIII, Chapters 61–3 |
| | XIX/XX, Chapters 64–7 |

Since the appearance of *Dickens at Work* (John Butt and Kathleen Tillotson, 1957), modern readers have become more aware of the importance of this form of publishing (begun more or less by accident with *Pickwick Papers*) as an influence on the construction of many novels of the period between 1837 and 1865. Publishing in numbers meant that the novelist was under constant pressure to produce manuscript for the forthcoming number, often with only a few days left at the end of the month to do it in. All novelists who used this system have left behind them harrowing stories of sudden panic and desperation. It required a constant effort and provided a constant stimulus to creative activity which Dickens always and Thackeray sometimes found beneficial. On the novel itself its influence was not always good. It meant that the unit of construction had to be the number rather than the chapter, and that the length of each unit was beyond the novelist's control. It helped to break down the dominance of a story plot in the novel, throwing the writer back on to other methods of unifying his work and encouraging the juxtaposition of scenes and character groups rather than sequential development such as was favoured by Sir Walter Scott (who would have been well suited to number publication). A glance at the endings of the numbers of *Vanity Fair* (for example, No. IX, Ch. 32) will show how well Thackeray adjusted to this system of publication, working up each number to a natural climax and exploiting to the full the emotional effect of delay, and will also serve as a reminder that it is in terms of the number rather than the chapter that the unity of *Vanity Fair* must be discussed.

SOME CRITICISMS OF 'VANITY FAIR'

Some modern readers evidently find it difficult to avoid associating Thackeray with one character or another. One argument asserts that Thackeray meant us to sympathise with Amelia; that Becky is more attractive to the modern reader than Amelia; and that therefore Thackeray failed in his intention except where Victorian readers were concerned, who were predisposed in Amelia's favour. Another has it that the intrinsically attractive Becky is made to act out of character in the later part of the novel when it is hinted that she poisons Jos Sedley. Yet another (often heard during the author's life-time) asserts that none of the

58

characters in the novel is worthy of the reader's admiration and that the 'sneering' of the narrator and the weakness of the characters create an impression of unwholesome cynicism rather than a healthy view of life. Many modern critics, affected by the theory of the novel which later emerged from the critical writings of Henry James, have declared that the novel violates a fundamental law of fiction in containing a breach between the realised story and the narrator/author who, in perpetually commenting on the characters and events, interferes with the author's main object—the creation of 'felt' or realised life. A reading of *Vanity Fair* which takes full account of its unique effect and of the subtle relationship between narrator and characters amounts to a refutal of each of these hostile assertions.

## THACKERAY'S DECLARED INTENTION

Thackeray's letters contain several comments which make quite clear the way in which he wished his readers to regard the characters of his story and provide definite evidence of his general purpose. A letter to his mother disposes of the idea that he meant Amelia to be the heroine of his *Novel without a Hero*:

> Of course you are quite right about Vanity Fair and Amelia being selfish. . . . My object is not to make a perfect character or anything like it. Don't you see how odious all the people are in the book (with exception of Dobbin)—behind whom all there lies a dark moral I hope. What I want is to make a set of people living without God in the world (only that is a cant phrase) greedy pompous mean perfectly self-satisfied for the most part and at ease about their superior virtue. Dobbin & poor Briggs are the only 2 people with real humility as yet. Amelia's is to come, when her scoundrel of a husband is well dead with a ball in his odious bowels; when she has had sufferings, a child, and a religion—But she has at present a quality above most people whizz: LOVE—by w$^h$ she shall be saved.
>
> Letter to his Mother, 2 July 1847

Eight months later he wrote to G. H. Lewes, who had reviewed *Vanity Fair* in the *Morning Chronicle*:

> I am quite aware of the dismal roguery w$^h$ goes all through the Vanity Fair story—and God forbid that the world should be like it

altogether: though I fear it is more like it than we like to own. But my object is to make every body engaged, engaged in the pursuit of Vanity and I must carry my story through in this dreary minor key, with only occasional hints here & there of better things—of better things w^h it does not become me to preach.

Letter to G. H. Lewes, 6 March 1848

To another critic, Robert Bell, who reviewed the novel in *Fraser's Magazine* for September 1848, he wrote with a more explicit answer to the charge of 'meanness':

If I had put in more fresh air as you call it my object would have been defeated—It is to indicate, in cheerful terms, that we are for the most part an abominably foolish and selfish people 'desperately wicked' and all eager after vanities. Everybody is you see in that book,—for instance if I had made Amelia a higher order of woman there would have been no vanity in Dobbins falling in love with her, whereas the impression at present is that he is a fool for his pains that he has married a silly little thing and in fact has found out his error rather a sweet and tender one however, *quia multum amavit* I want to leave everybody dissatisfied and unhappy at the end of the story—we ought all to be with our own and all other stories. Good God dont I see (in that may-be cracked and warped looking glass in which I am always looking) my own weaknesses wickednesses lusts follies shortcomings? in company let us hope with better qualities about which we will pretermit discourse. We must lift up our voices about these and howl to a congregation of fools: so much at least has been my endeavour. You have all of you taken my misanthropy to task—I wish I could myself: but take the world by a certain standard (you know what I mean) and who dares talk of having any virtue at all? Letter to R. Bell, 3 September 1848

These comments help us to dispose of several of the misunderstandings which have grown up around the novel and to start making an accurate assessment of the moral statement involved in it.

### AMELIA AND BECKY

*Vanity Fair*, as many critics have pointed out, is partly based on the contrast between the two women whose fortunes we follow from the time of their entry into the world (aged sixteen and nineteen respectively) to their eventual establishment, apparently beyond the reach of further fluctuations of fortune, eighteen years later. Many novels have been formed in superficially similar fashion—Jane Austen's *Sense and Sensibility* and Mrs. Gaskell's *Wives and Daughters* are two obvious examples—but *Vanity Fair* differs from most of them in not encouraging the reader to make a straightforward qualitative contrast between the two 'heroines'.

Even without the authoritative comments of Thackeray in his letters the reader should be able to perceive in the novel itself that the contrast results, for the most part, in showing us two ways of being 'vain' (in the biblical sense of 'futile' or 'worthless'). In *Vanity Fair*, as in much of his earlier work, Thackeray was attacking the ideas and patterns involved in the fiction of his time and particularly the concepts of the ideal and the heroic (in the novel writer's sense), insisting on an analysis of character and motivation which revealed a degree of selfishness in almost every human action. The difference between Amelia and Becky is not that between a good woman and a bad but that between a selfishly good one and a selfishly bad. The criterion which makes judgment possible in spite of this is based on the capacity to love, which can lead to unselfishness and an escape from Vanity. Amelia has this capacity, though for the greater part of the action it is warped by her silliness and refusal to think about the people around her. Becky never has it and this is why Thackeray disapproves of her.

Criticism of Thackeray's treatment of Becky has often rested on a misunderstanding of two important factors—the nature of her 'guilt' towards her husband and the essential coarseness of her nature, which means that she requires constant stimulation of a not very admirable kind. Becky is an attractive character because she is refreshingly active and lively in contrast to the passive and uninteresting Amelia, and refreshingly natural in contrast to the self-righteous and hypocritical characters like Mrs. Bute Crawley, Lady Southdown and Lady Blanche Gaunt. These contrasts make her by far the most interesting character in the first half of the novel, when she is fighting a battle for social acceptance against people no better and less able than herself. The turning-point in our assessment of her character comes in the middle of the novel when we begin to appreciate the character of her husband.

Rawdon Crawley begins the novel as a stupid and dishonest dragoon, trading on his skill at games of chance and his social position in order to fleece those people whose vanity puts them in his power. At first something of a likeness to Algernon Deuceace, he only begins to win our sympathy when he begins to show his essential simplicity and his ability to give affection. The scene at Brussels before and during the Battle of Waterloo makes this aspect of his character clear. The sincerity and affection which he shows in making the inventory of his property before going to battle is contrasted with that of George Osborne, selfish to the last. A little later Thackeray makes a deliberate contrast between Amelia and Becky, bringing in Mrs. O'Dowd to extend the comparison and to make sure that we appreciate the frigid selfishness of the one and the self-centred weakness of the other. The fact that he uses the comic O'Dowds for this purpose emphasises the extent to which he is concerned to make a roughly realistic portrayal of human nature. The scene which depicts their behaviour on the night before the battle is touching; they show virtues of a high order; yet their comedy is unimpaired.

The next major advance in the revelation of Becky's character comes in the chapters around the great scene in which Rawdon escapes from the sponging house and finds his wife in intimate *tête-à-tête* with Lord Steyne. As has been frequently observed, Thackeray leaves the question of whether or not Becky committed adultery with Lord Steyne unsettled, though he gives us enough information to allow us to form our own conclusions. Again, towards the end of the novel, in Chapter 64, when he is accounting for her activities after leaving England and before reappearing in Germany, he is reticent, working through innuendo rather than by direct statement. The implication is clear enough—that during her 'vagabond' wanderings when she associated with the scum of European society, Becky had behaved with no regard for morals—but the statement is very indirect. Thackeray attributes this to the prudery of his readers:

> We must pass over a part of Mrs. Rebecca Crawley's biography
> with that lightness and delicacy which the world demands—the
> moral world, that has, perhaps, no particular objection to vice, but
> an insuperable repugnance to hearing vice called by its proper name.
>
> VANITY FAIR 64

For this and other similar passages Thackeray has been accused of
coyness, of playing with the subject of adultery and prostitution.
But elsewhere in his work he is by no means as squeamish as he
appears to be here, as a reading of *Men's Wives, Barry Lyndon* or
*Catherine* will immediately show. The main reason for his refusal
to commit himself to direct statement about what Becky had
done during the later part of her life was that it did not take place
within the framework of the social world with which he was
dealing, and did not involve her selfish seeking after vanity.

The earlier incident is somewhat different and Thackeray does
make sure that he is in control of our emotional response,
suggesting far more than he states. The 'wretched woman . . .
clung hold of his coat, of his hands; her own were all covered
with serpents, and rings, and baubles.' The idea of the serpent
extends to Steyne, who, 'almost strangled . . . writhed and bent'
in Rawdon's grasp and is flung to the ground. The biblical echoes
of the scene have been mentioned by several critics.

Rawdon never answers Becky's insistent statement, 'I am
innocent, Rawdon . . . before God I am innocent'. The real issue
for him is not the dubious one of adultery but the actual and
undeniable one of betrayal and deceit. Number XV, of which the
chapter describing the confrontation is the third and last, is constructed so as to isolate this betrayal from the rest of the action
and to provide a commentary on it. The three chapters are: 51,
*In Which a Charade is Acted . . .*; 52, *In Which Lord Steyne Shows
himself in a most Amiable Light*; and 53, *A Rescue and a Catastrophe*.
The first of these, containing the charade, is in effect a prefiguring
of the last, in which Becky acts out the part of Clytemnestra to
Rawdon's Agamemnon. The second charade, to the reader aware
of the myth of Philomela, the innocent maiden raped and muti-
lated by Tereus, is (in the light of the Clytemnestra episode) an
ironical comment on Becky's 'theatrical youth' and equally

theatrical innocence. The chapter ends with the apparently co-incidental arrest of Rawdon as he walks with Steyne's creature Wenham. In the next chapter (52) Thackeray breaks the sequence of action and describes the events leading up to the night of the charades and Steyne's gradual elimination of all the people around Becky who could impede the consummation of his relationship with her—first her son, then Briggs and lastly Raw-don himself. The end of the chapter makes a direct connection between Rawdon's growing disquiet about the relationship between Becky and Steyne and the arrest itself:

> And it was while Rawdon's mind was agitated with these doubts and perplexities that the incident occurred which was mentioned in the last Chapter; and the unfortunate Colonel found himself a prisoner away from home.                                   52

Readers who have appreciated the extent of Becky's betrayal of Rawdon and understood the degree to which she is frigid and selfish have sometimes been unable to accept her behaviour after her fall, or the suggestion that she murdered Jos Sedley. Lord David Cecil, for example, in his *Early Victorian Novelists* (1934), argues that the suggestion that Becky murders Jos is improbable and out of character, because murders in 19th-century England took place only among the officially criminal classes and the neurotic. Apart from the fact that the murder takes place not in England but on the Continent, it certainly does not take place in civilised society but, as Thackeray makes quite clear, in a world of sordid and sinister Bohemianism into which Jos has been dragged and in which he is trapped.

And this is the world to which Becky, by natural sympathy, belongs. It is noticeable that Thackeray does not tell us all about her origins at once. He refrains from compromising his 'heroine' at the beginning of the story, only revealing certain facts about her (such as her illegitimacy) when her character has started to show of its own accord, throwing out hints from time to time about her 'dismal precocity', her experience in flirtation, her knowledge of the world, and making it abundantly clear that her social striving is only one manifestation of the need for stimulation, another of which is the brandy bottle. Becky's own suggestion that if she had £5,000 a year she could be virtuous is a dubious one in the light of her inability to restrain herself for any length of time in the various virtuous but dull households in which she finds herself.

The moral pattern of the novel in which Becky and Amelia play such large parts is fairly clear. The object of Thackeray's strongest attack is selfishness, the only way of avoiding it being the development of an ability to feel affection for other people. The capacity for unselfish action is the final criterion by which the characters are to be judged (in so far, that is, as they are to be judged at all). Dobbin and Miss Briggs are the only characters who are unselfish. Rawdon and Amelia both come to feel more for others than they feel for themselves, his affection for his son growing the more as he becomes alienated from his wife. Lady Jane Crawley, the wife of the younger Sir Pitt, plays an important part in the 'taming' of the dragoon and she is one of the characters who relieve the predominant atmosphere of 'roguery' which Thackeray mentioned in his letter to Lewes. Amelia is treated in no gentle fashion. She awakens the narrator's sentimental response when she innocently and unselfishly adores George Osborne, but after his death the narrator's attitude changes. The turning point in his (and our) assessment of her character comes during the scenes at Brussels when she leans so heavily on Peggy O'Dowd, whose husband is in the same danger as her own. Later we come to realise that she is transferring her adoration from George to his son and treating him almost as a god, helping to make him into a creature as arrogant, selfish and worthless as his father. At the same time Thackeray balances our growing awareness of her selfishness in rejecting Dobbin and in indulging in sentimental image worship by a full description of her charity towards her spiteful mother and her father, whose financial irresponsibility was the cause of her having to part with Georgey to his paternal grandfather. Amelia's suffering is adequate compensation to the reader for her selfishness and silliness.

This is only so, however, up to the time when Jos Sedley and Dobbin return from India, the latter not fully recovered from an illness brought on by the violence of his reaction to an insensitive letter from her. When Dobbin returns he and the reader begin to realise the full extent of Amelia's selfishness. When her material condition is improved she is no longer a victim, and with Dobbin at hand she becomes a tyrant, finally, in the callous rejection of his claim on her affection, showing him that she was not worth the love which he had offered. Dobbin tells Amelia:

> I know what your heart is capable of . . . it can't feel such an attachment as mine deserves to mate with, and such as I would have won from a woman more generous than you. No, you are not worthy of the love which I have devoted to you. I knew all along that the prize I had set my life on was not worth the winning; that I was a fool, with fond fancies, too, bartering away my all of truth and ardour against your little feeble remnant of love. I will bargain no more: I withdraw. I find no fault with you. You are very good-natured, and have done your best; but you couldn't—you couldn't reach up to the height of the attachment which I bore you, and which a loftier soul than yours might have been proud to share. Goodbye, Amelia! I have watched your struggle. Let it end. We are both weary of it. 66

Amelia calls Dobbin back because she realises that she needs him, even before Becky reveals to her how wrong she has been, but Thackeray's words at the end of the novel leave us with the knowledge that the complete love which he had once had for her never returned.

We cannot rest at the end of *Vanity Fair* with the image of any ideal relationship, or with the sense of an ideal completeness of any kind. Even Dobbin, as the narrator points out, is a 'spooney' and even Lady Jane is weak and narrow-minded. The novel-reader's ideal is deflated even with the very last words:

> Ah! Vanitas Vanitatum! which of us is happy in this world? which of us has his desire? or, having it, is satisfied?—Come children, let us shut up the box and the puppets, for our play is played out. 67

Yet there is more behind the last paragraph than the desire to achieve deflation of the normal expectations of the novel reader. In this passage Thackeray takes up the stance which he first assumed in the preface to the novel, 'Before the Curtain', where he put himself forward as the Manager of a theatrical performance in a booth in Vanity Fair, referring to the characters in the novel as puppets and admitting to the presence of an element of melodrama in the tale:

> He is proud to think that his Puppets have given satisfaction to the very best company in this empire. The famous little Becky Puppet has been pronounced to be uncommonly flexible in the joints, and lively on the wires . . . the Little Boy's Dance has been liked by some; and please to remark the richly dressed figure of the Wicked Nobleman, on which no expense has been spared, and which Old Nick will fetch away at the end of this singular performance.
>
> VANITY FAIR, 'BEFORE THE CURTAIN'

Those who have held with Ford Madox Ford that the object of the novelist is to create such an illusion of reality that the reader forgets that he is reading a novel have objected to Thackeray's suggestion that the characters are puppets rather than people, and to the constant intrusion of the narrator between the reader and the characters and events which he describes. Such a reader, who objects in principle to the device of the intrusive narrator and who reads *Vanity Fair* as if it ought to consist of the story alone, will not be in a position to interpret the novel as it actually is—and he will inevitably fall short of understanding the very subtle effect which Thackeray wanted to achieve.

Interpretation of *Vanity Fair* depends on an understanding of the relationship between Thackeray (as author), the narrator, and the events and characters of the story. The mistake of confusing Thackeray with his narrator is an elementary one, but one that can be made by quite sophisticated critics. Dorothy Van Ghent, in *The English Novel: Form and Function* (1953), is a good example, objecting to the idea of Thackeray himself intruding in the novel and pulling the characters out of the fictional world by speaking of them in relationship to himself. That the narrator and Thackeray are not to be identified is obvious from the facts which we learn about him in the course of his narration—that he was young fifty years ago, that his boyhood occurred twenty-five years ago, and that he has a wealthy maiden aunt and a wife called Julia!

In which case, several questions remain: for what purpose did Thackeray create him and put his personality between the reader and the story, and to what extent does he represent the official voice of the author? These questions are of central importance and must be answered before criticism as pointed as that of Dorothy Van Ghent can be answered and full understanding of the novel achieved.

### REALISATION IN 'VANITY FAIR'

With regard to the most basic criticism which Dorothy Van Ghent puts forward and which has frequently been made—that the narrator interferes between the reader and the created world of the characters—the obvious and easy answer is that the narrator is as much a part of the created world as Becky Sharp or Rawdon Crawley. If he is not Thackeray himself, who is he but a character? Thackeray took care, towards the end of the novel, to put the narrator into the world which he was describing by making him give an account of his original meeting with the people whose story he has been telling. Elsewhere, outside the novel, he insisted on the importance of realisation and vivid representation with an emphasis worthy of his critics. Thus, he wrote to David Masson to the effect that Art is not Art *rather than* Nature, insisting that 'the Art of Novels is to represent Nature; to convey as strongly as possible the sentiment of reality' (see above, p. 10). Indeed, the very critics who have objected to his 'spoiling' the impression of life have done so on the grounds that what is spoilt is a quality of realisation seldom exceeded by other novelists. In his own day Thackeray was said to have done more for the establishment of realism in the novel than any other writer; it is ironic that he should since have been criticised for destroying what he created.

The narrator—who, after all, is as finely realised as Becky Sharp!—is a part of the created world of *Vanity Fair*, but his relationship with the reader is different from that of the other characters who stand at a farther remove. By virtue of his vivid realisation Thackeray created two dimensions, putting the narrator in a position from which he can withdraw out of sight and hearing at important moments in the story, taking the liberty at times of stepping forward to join the puppets, at others of stepping back and joining us.

The question of what Thackeray intended to effect by creating this intrusive narrator is bound up with the other question of why he chose, in the preface and throughout the novel, to stress the fact that the characters were puppets in a puppet show which was being played in a world which was not the world of the narrator and the contemporary reader. The answer to both questions is to be found in the work of Thomas Carlyle.

The cover of the original parts of *Vanity Fair* bore a design of a narrator, in motley and a long-eared cap, standing on an upturned tub and addressing an audience as long-eared as himself (see illustrations). Both Kathleen Tillotson and Thackeray's biographer, Gordon Ray, have pointed out that this design is a reference to a passage in Carlyle's essay *On Biography*, published in *Fraser's Magazine* in 1832. Carlyle attacked the emptiness of contemporary novels but qualified his attack by saying that even the worst of them might contain something:

> Of no given book, not even a Fashionable Novel, can you predicate with certainty that its vacuity is absolute; that there are not other vacuities which shall partially replenish themselves therefrom, and esteem it a *plenum*. How knowest thou, may the distressed Novelwright exclaim, that I, here where I sit, am the Foolishest of existing mortals; that this my Long-ear of a Fictitious Biography shall not find one and the other, into whose still longer ears it may be the means, under Providence, of instilling somewhat? We answer None knows, none can certainly know: therefore, write on, worthy Brother, even as thou canst, even as it has been given thee.
>
> Thomas Carlyle, ON BIOGRAPHY 1832

Thackeray refers to this passage again in Chapter 8 of *Vanity Fair* when he is speaking of the 'humbugs and falsenesses and pretensions' which abound in Vanity Fair and about which even he, the long-eared narrator of a novel, must be truthful.

It does not seem to have been suggested that there is more behind

Thackeray's reference to Carlyle's essay than a mock-modest protest of his own seriousness of purpose. But in Carlyle's essay on J. W. Croker's edition of Boswell's *Life of Johnson*, to which the essay *On Biography* was meant to serve as a preface, there is a passage which suggests a much deeper relationship than this. In this passage Carlyle speaks of great men and contrasts them with ordinary people:

> . . . while others hovered and swam along, in the grand Vanity-Fair of the world, blinded by the mere Shows of things, these saw into the Things themselves, and could walk as men having an eternal lode star and with their feet on sure paths. Thus was there a *Reality* in their existence; something of a perennial character; in virtue of which indeed it is that the memory of them is perennial. Whoso belongs only to his own age, and reverences only *its* gilt Popinjays or soot-smeared Mumbo jumbos, must needs die with it: though he have been crowned seven times in the Capitol . . . there was nothing universal, nothing eternal in him; he must fade away, even as the Popinjay-gildings and Scarecrow-apparel, which he could not see through.
>
> Thomas Carlyle, BOSWELL'S LIFE OF JOHNSON 1832

Thackeray told us that the title of *Vanity Fair* came to him during the night with no warning and no apparent associations, but it is not necessary that we should attempt to prove that a passage which he must have read was in his mind when he wrote the novel. The important thing is that this passage from Carlyle suggests the most basic intention that Thackeray had in writing *Vanity Fair*.

'Vanity' in this novel is not to be taken as having simply a biblical reference such as that which we see in Bunyan's *Pilgrim's Progress* where the idea of the Fair originated. The word refers to a concept fundamentally allied to that which is involved in the passage from Carlyle—it suggests that those who seek it are fundamentally godless and are living their lives without directing their energies in a fruitful way. According to Carlyle's interpretation of life, Amelia would be a creature who was seeking after Vanity because she worshipped something unreal, and Dobbin would be so because he sought for happiness and expected to find it by means of another human being.

This leads us to the explanation of why Thackeray spoke of his characters as puppets rather than as men and women—because according to the attitude to life which his reading of Carlyle had helped him to, none of the characters acquire the status of human beings; all are puppets in a very real sense, driven by their own desires rather than purposefully seeking an object worthy of the devotion of complete men and women. From time to time certain of them realise the direction in which they are being impelled and have sufficient strength of character, to alter their course. For others an essential poverty of nature makes it impossible to do anything but hover and swim along on the tide of their own desires.

The contrast between the two old men, John Sedley and John Osborne, provides examples of both types. The former, once his success has been taken from him, loses the personality which went with it and becomes a pathetic failure, weakly and vainly struggling to regain financial prosperity and the identity which he has irrevocably lost. Like his former friend and benefactor, old Osborne equates personal identity with financial prosperity and by doing so he involves himself in a vicious circle of events which pains no one more than himself, but he has enough strength of character to save himself. When George marries Amelia, old Osborne makes a ritual sacrifice of his son to the passion of pride. In the scene which shows him crossing his son's name out of the Bible and burning his letters he anticipates the actual death of George on the battlefield. Thackeray ends the scene with a contrast between the death-dealing father and the signs of a reawakening of life outside:

> It was morning already: as he went up to bed, the whole house was alight with the sunshine; and the birds were singing among the fresh green leaves in Russell Square.                                    24

After his son's death Osborne becomes even more a victim of his own contending passions, the inner conflict between love, pride, hatred and selfishness causing a degree and kind of feeling which shocks the sergeant who escorts him round the battle-field of Waterloo. Only his love for the child of Amelia and George allows him to approach salvation and to break out of the circle in which he is trapped.

William Dobbin, who makes an image for himself and worships it, admitting at the end of the story that the process involved a measure of self-deceit, falls into the same category of those who chain themselves to their own 'gilt Popinjay'. Ironically the process by which he frees himself helps Amelia to free herself from the pattern of idol worship, the falsity of which is underlined for us by Thackeray's frequent reference to George's painted image. Jos Sedley is trapped in a different way, but more surely trapped. Even Becky suffers the frustration involved in the attempted manufacture of a *persona* which she has not the material advantage to make acceptable nor the character to enjoy. Her ultimate 'respectability' is the very reverse of what she had aimed at through the novel and the only possible and appropriate compensation for the totally artificial life which she had tried to create.

That the characters of *Vanity Fair* are manipulated by their own desires and impulses, 'living without God in the world' and 'blinded by the mere shows of things', makes it dramatically appropriate that they should be manipulated by a narrator who is aware of their hollowness. But the use of the narrator also gives Thackeray other advantages. The freedom of commentary allows him to widen and deepen the reference of his story.

THE 'TEXTURE' OF 'VANITY FAIR'

The thickness of texture in this novel has often been commented on. *Vanity Fair* is full of characters, scenes and references which form an intricate web of reality, tying the story to the context of Regency England, Regency England to Victorian England, the present of the narrator to the past of the characters and to the present of his readers. The story takes place during the period immediately before and for some years after the Battle of Waterloo (1815). The personality of the narrator, who speaks to us in the present tense, widens the reference of the story, an effect which

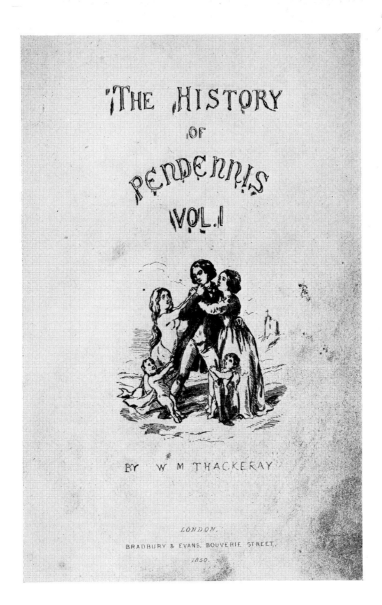

The title-page of *The History of Pendennis* drawn by Thackeray.

FLORE ET ZEPHYR

*Ballet Mythologique*

DÉDIÉ
À

par    *Théophile Wagstaff*

LONDON PUBLISHED MARCH 1836 BY J. MITCHELL LIBRARY, 33 OLD BOND ST

The title-page of *Flore et Zephyr* drawn by Thackeray.

# THE NEWCOMES

## MEMOIRS OF A MOST Respectable FAMILY

EDITED BY

## ARTHUR PENDENNIS ESQ<sup>r</sup>

IN TWO VOLUMES.

VOL. I.

NEW YORK:

HARPER & BROTHERS, PUBLISHERS,

PEARL STREET, FRANKLIN SQUARE.

1856.

The title-page of *The Newcomes* (not drawn by Thackeray).

Thackeray's designs for the cover of *Vanity Fair*.

is increased again by passages like that which introduces the Crawley family, extending the time sequence even farther into an indefinitely distant past of Vanity-seeking:

> Sir Pitt Crawley (named after the great Commoner) was the son of Walpole Crawley, first Baronet, of the Tape and Sealing-Wax Office in the reign of George II, when he was impeached for peculation, as were a great number of other honest gentlemen of those days; and Walpole Crawley was, as need scarcely be said, son of John Churchill Crawley, named after the celebrated military commander of the reign of Queen Anne. The family tree (which hangs up at Queen's Crawley) furthermore mentions Charles Stuart, afterwards called Barebones Crawley, son of the Crawley of James the First's time; and finally, Queen Elizabeth's Crawley, who is represented as the foreground of the picture in his forked beard and armour. 7

A somewhat similar effect is achieved by the names of the characters in the novel—Crawley, Southdown, Stubble, Bunny are all indications of Thackeray's ability to typify the individual and to capture in a way unobtrusive enough to pass in a real world suggestions of the universal and timeless moral which lies somewhere behind the action. The device is at its most striking in the roll of titles which is given in the account of the death of the Marquis of Steyne, a list which rises through parody of newspaper obituary to the universality of allegory:

> . . . the Most Honourable George Gustavus, Marquis of Steyne, Earl of Gaunt and of Gaunt Castle, in the Peerage of Ireland, Viscount Hellborough, Baron Pitchley and Grillsby, a Knight of the Most Noble Order of the Garter, of the Golden Fleece of Spain, of the Russian Order of Saint Nicholas of the First Class, of the Turkish Order of the Crescent, First Lord of the Powder Closet and Groom of the Back Stairs, Colonel of the Gaunt or Regent's Own Regiment of Militia, a Trustee of the British Museum, an Elder Brother of the Trinity House, a Governor of the White Friars, and D.C.L. . . . 64

One of the most fascinating aspects of *Vanity Fair* is the impression it gives of the interpenetration of the representational and the real. The title of the novel, the moral pattern involved, the system of contrasts, the persistent impulse towards typification revealed in the naming of the characters—all these things are closely interwoven with the many references to topical events, social events, popular songs and performers, and historical personages (the Marquis of Steyne was obviously modelled on the Marquis of Hertford), and exist in a context of human behaviour vividly realised. And one of the major factors binding them together is the personality of the narrator.

The narrator also makes possible a widening of the scope of the novel in a somewhat different way. He is, in his own words, often introduced 'to personify the world in general'. So when Becky's disappointment at missing marriage with Sir Pitt by her premature marriage to his son is in question, the narrator explains her feelings by reference to his own experiences in Vanity Fair:

> I remember one night being in the Fair myself, at an evening party. I observed old Miss Toady, there also present, single out for her special attentions and flattery little Mrs. Briefless, the barrister's wife, who is of a good family certainly, but, as we all know, is as poor as poor can be. . . . If the mere chance of becoming a baronet's daughter can procure a lady such homage in the world, surely, surely we may respect the agonies of a young woman who has lost the opportunity of becoming a baronet's wife.  15

At other times the presence of the narrator allows Thackeray to achieve in the use of symbol a complexity of effect and humour which is rarely obtainable by more straightforward means. He uses his symbols with deliberate obviousness in order to achieve a calculated effect. Such occasions arise whenever he refers to the clock surmounted by a group representing the sacrifice of Iphigenia by her father before the Grecian fleet at Aulis. The clock stands on the mantelpiece in the drawing-room of Osborne's house in Russell Square and is used to achieve indirect humorous comment on the actions which take place beneath it. The first instance is when Osborne returns from the City with the information that Amelia's father is about to be declared a bankrupt and that the marriage between her and George will have to be stopped:

> . . . this worthy man lapsed into his particular chair, and then the utter silence in his genteel, well-furnished drawing-room was only interrupted by the alarmed ticking of the great French clock.

> When that chronometer, which was surmounted by a cheerful brass group of the sacrifice of Iphigenia, tolled five in a heavy cathedral tone, Mr. Osborne pulled the bell at his right hand violently, and the butler rushed up. 13

At this point the sacrifice referred to is that of Amelia. Later the reference is more subtle, when Dobbin comes to see Miss Osborne in order to tell her that George and Amelia are married:

> ... the Captain and Miss Osborne were left together. They were both so silent that the tick-tock of the Sacrifice of Iphigenia clock on the mantlepiece became quite rudely audible. 23

Here it is impossible to be certain whose sacrifice is referred to; Jane thinks that Dobbin is going to propose to her and is ready to render herself, but the reader's anxieties are centred on Dobbin. Later still the clock clearly refers to the lonely and miserable Jane Osborne who has been sacrificed to her father's comfort, though partly by her own consent:

> At half-past nine he rose and went to the City, and she was almost free till dinner-time, to make visitations in the kitchen, and to scold the servants: to drive abroad and descend upon the tradesmen, who were prodigiously respectful: to leave her cards and her papa's at the great glum respectable houses of City Friends; or to sit alone in the large drawing-room, expecting visitors; and working at a huge piece of worsted by the fire, on the sofa, hard by the great Iphigenia clock, which ticked and tolled with mournful loudness in the dreary room. 42

In all these passages we are aware of the voice of the narrator and of his controlling influence. The characters are not aware of the clock or of its significance and we are not encouraged to think of it too seriously as a symbol of the action in which they are engaged. The idea of sacrifice is there in all the scenes and we are made very aware of it without being permitted to forget that it is in no way a tragic sacrifice. Thackeray wants us to keep our distance, observing rather than participating.

In *Vanity Fair* we are not always conscious of the narrator, but there is never any attempt made to make us forget that he is in charge of the story. The great scenes are delivered as 'great scenes', are part of the showmanship of the narrator and something in which he takes a proper pride. He is even aware of—and makes sure that we are aware of—the periodic climaxes which the novel owes to the fact of its being published in parts. He plays with the reader's involvement and curiosity, commenting on various ways of relating the events and sometimes deliberately holding back information or giving it before, in the 'normal' course of events, it would have become due. Throughout the novel there is a tension between our sense that the story is going on before us, in its own present tense, and our sense that only the telling is going on before us, the story having occurred in the past.

This tension was the result of Thackeray's most basic intention in writing the novel. He wanted to create the impression that while the present of the characters and their actions was real and substantial, yet it was, in another sense, unreal and insubstantial. The miseries of the characters are very real to them, but according to the terminology found in the work of Carlyle to which Thackeray refers us they are no more than shadows, their world no more than an empty show. Sedley's pathetic attempts to restore himself; Amelia's grief for George; Osborne's frustrated love; Becky's dilemma of being forced by her own desires to seek something which cannot satisfy her: all these things are the result of a basic failure in the characters who inhabit Vanity Fair to free themselves from the domination of their own desires and to adjust themselves to reality. Consequently Thackeray put the narrator between the characters and the reader and used him just as he used other devices of style and construction to create his novel, a glittering, shifting and yet ultimately most solid masterpiece.

# 5

# 'Pendennis'

The success of *Vanity Fair* changed the course of Thackeray's career. He continued writing for *Punch* and contributing from time to time to other periodicals and annuals. He also continued to publish Christmas Books—extended and illustrated sketches directed at a family audience. *Mrs. Perkins' Ball* (1847) was the first of these, followed by *Our Street* (1848), *Dr. Birch and his Young Friends* (1849), *The Kickleburys on the Rhine* (1850), and *The Rose and the Ring* (1855). But the most important aspect of his career between 1848 and 1860, when he accepted the editorship of the *Cornhill Magazine*, was the publication of four full-length novels, on which depended his status as a major novelist and the only rival of Charles Dickens.

The first of these novels was *The History of Pendennis, His Fortunes and Misfortunes, His Friends and His Greatest Enemy*, which came out in numbers between November 1848 and December 1850. More or less at the same time (1849–50) Dickens's *David Copperfield* was appearing and to some extent comparison of the two novels is inevitable. Both are *Bildungsromane*, or novels which portray the growth from youth to manhood of a central character, and into both are woven sensational elements relating to the fate of characters other than the hero. Both novels are concerned with selfishness and materialism and both contain a central incident bearing on the seduction (in *David Copperfield*) or near seduction (in *Pendennis*) of a girl from the lower classes by a gentleman. The most superficial reading of the two novels indicates the extent of the considerable differences between the two writers. There is no question of imitation or influence of one on the other, although Thackeray may have been right in thinking that the new simplicity of Dickens's style was perhaps in some measure the result of the impact of *Vanity Fair*. The import-ance of the similarity lies in the fact that the subject of the growth from innocence through selfishness to maturity was a common one in Victorian literature because it allowed of the treatment of certain questions which were felt to be basic to the moral and intellectual conditions of the time. It is no coincidence that in the very first number of *Pendennis* Thackeray makes a reference to a poem which Victorian readers thought of as stating most accur-ately one of the central problems of the age—Wordsworth's *Ode On Intimations of Immortality*:

> I don't say that the boy is lost, or that the innocence has left him which he had from 'Heaven, which is our home,' but that the shades of the prison-house are closing very fast over him, and that we are helping as much as possible to corrupt him.      PENDENNIS 2

While he was writing the novel he wrote to Arthur Hugh Clough to express his delight with the latter's poem, *The Bothie of Tober na Vuolich*, and told him:

> I have been going over some of the same ground (of youth) in this present number of Pendennis: w^h I fear will be considered rather warm by the puritans: but I think you'll understand it—that is if you care for such trivialities, or take the trouble to look under the stream of the story.    Letter to Arthur Clough, 24 November 1848

The rest of Clough's poetry, which deals explicitly and directly with the problems arising from the mid-Victorian intellectual position, problems about the possibility of Faith and the associa-tion of growth with materialistic pressure and moral compromise, may almost be taken as a parallel statement to that which lies under the stream of the story of *Pendennis*. Clough himself suffered, and depicted his heroes as having suffered, from the same moral disease which attacks Arthur Pendennis. The extent to which Thackeray meant Pen's case to be seen as a general one is indicated by the fact that he makes him refer to the brothers, John Henry and Francis Newman, who began their lives as Protestants and ended them in the opposing camps of the Roman Catholics and the Rationalists. Pen's reference is a succinct statement of what this contrast meant to Victorian readers:

> I see . . . [the truth] in that man, who, driven fatally by the remorse-
> less logic of his creed, gives up everything . . . and passes over,
> truth-impelled, to the enemy, in whose ranks he is ready to serve
> henceforth as a nameless private soldier:—I see the truth in that man,
> as I do in his brother, whose logic drives him to a quite different
> conclusion. . . . If the truth is with all these, why should I take side
> with any one of them?                                                     61

The frontispiece to Volume I of *Pendennis* (see illustrations)
makes the theme of the novel clear from the start. It depicts a
young man clasped in the embrace of two females, each of whom
is pulling him towards her. One of them is a dark-haired girl,
around whose waist the young man has his arm and who is
assisted by a small winged cupid. The other is a mermaid, her tail
peeping coyly from under the drapery which covers the lower
parts of her body, who is assisted by a diminutive devil with
horns and cloven hooves but apparently no tail. The hero is sus-
pended between two conflicting states, on the one side destructive worldliness (we remember the habits of mermaids from
Chapter 64 of *Vanity Fair*), on the other, domestic affection.

MAJOR PENDENNIS AS MERMAID!

It is tempting to identify the dark-haired maiden of the illustration with Laura Bell and the mermaid with the fair-haired
Blanche Amory, because to some extent the two girls do represent
the conflicting claims suggested in the illustration. But the mermaid's chief representative in *Pendennis* is the superannuated
half-pay Major, Arthur's uncle, who stands in opposition to his
loving, pure-hearted but narrow-minded sister-in-law, Helen
Pendennis. These two politely manœuvre for control over the
mind of the easily led Arthur Pendennis, our sympathy shifting
with the stream of events. Thackeray does not attempt to portray
either of them as simply good or bad, entirely deserving of the
reader's approval. *Pendennis*, like all his other novels, suggests a
reading of human nature which takes full account of the disturb-
ing mixture of motives which lies behind the actions of the main

characters. We are able to assess both the Major and Helen Pendennis objectively, to see clearly when either of them is right or wrong, and to understand the full circumstances of their being so. The old man is worldly and small-minded, placing social success and the opinion of equals and superiors above the domestic virtues and the higher moral qualities. Yet he is by no means a despicable character. It is his worldly wisdom which allows Pen to escape from the trap in which both Warrington and Bell (Laura's father) were caught, and to avoid what would have been the disastrous marriage with Emily Costigan, twelve years his senior and much his inferior in social status, education and sensitivity. At several points in the action, when he has sunk low in the estimation of the reader, the sudden manifestation of some quality like bravery or generosity raises him again and reminds us that neither he nor the attitude which he represents is to be easily dismissed. His treatment of Captain Costigan at the beginning of the novel, his courage and self-possession in dealing with the scoundrelly valet, Morgan, and the generosity which he shows to the latter's victim, Mrs. Brixham, are instances of this kind. His influence on Arthur is not entirely bad in its effects, being a healthy counter-balance to the sentimental spirituality of the boy's mother. We see him at his worst after the entertainment at Lord Steyne's where he has been dancing attendance on Lady Clavering and Blanche Amory in order to further his plan of marrying Pen to Blanche. The large element of selfishness which is mixed up with his attempt to benefit his nephew makes his appearance in the morning and the agony which he has suffered during the night finely comic. The original edition of the novel had a half-page illustration of the Major after the night's 'entertainment' which underlines the effect of Thackeray's merciless description of his appearance. But even at this point we are not permitted to think too simply of the Major. His object was worthless, his sufferings comic, but as Thackeray insists:

> If a man, struggling with hardship and bravely overcoming it, is an object of admiration for the gods, that Power in whose chapels the old Major was a faithful worshipper must have looked upwards approvingly upon the constancy of Pendennis's martyrdom. There

are sufferers in that cause as in the other: the negroes in the service of Mumbo Jumbo tattoo and drill themselves with burning skewers with great fortitude; and we read that the priests in the service of Baal gashed themselves and bled freely. You who can smash the idols, do so with a good courage; but do not be too fierce with the idolaters,—they worship the best thing they know.            45

The Major's affection for his nephew is not strong enough to impinge on his inveterate selfishness to a sufficient extent to permit him to risk a visit when Pen has a possibly contagious fever. He is satisfied with transacting his benevolence 'by deputy and post', but he is never so hardened that his affection cannot break through the shell of selfishness. The world which he adores, of which the Marquis of Steyne is, if not the deity, the very highest priest, can be shattered by the force of something more real than itself. In the scene at Stillbrook when the news of Pen's danger is brought to the Major, the presence of an old man's grief permits, for a moment, the recognition of something higher than the usages of the social world:

> Wagg said, 'It's a bailiff come down to nab the Major;' but nobody laughed at the pleasantry.
>
> 'Hullo! What's the matter, Pendennis?' cried Lord Steyne, with his strident voice. 'Anything wrong?'
>
> 'It's—it's—my boy that's *dead*,' said the Major, and burst into a sob—the old man was quite overcome.
>
> 'Not dead, my Lord; but very ill when I left London,' Mr. Bows said, in a low voice.
>
> A britzka came up at this moment as the three men were speaking. The peer looked at his watch. 'You've twenty minutes to catch the mail-train. Jump in, Pendennis; and drive like h——, sir, do you hear?'
>
> The carriage drove off swiftly with Pendennis and his companion, and let us trust that the oath will be pardoned to the Marquis of Steyne.            51

THE SIDE OF THE ANGELS

Helen Pendennis's deep love for her son and instinctive turning away from anything corrupt or 'worldly' are much to be admired. But just as Major Pendennis was presented as a complex figure, and even the Marquis of Steyne shown to have human feelings and respect for grief, so she is portrayed with all the defects of a fully-conceived human being. One of her faults is revealed at the outset of the novel:

> That even a woman should be faultless . . . is an arrangement not permitted by nature, which assigns to us mental defects, as it awards to us headaches, illnesses, or death: without which the scheme of the world could not be carried on,—nay, some of the best qualities of mankind could not be brought into exercise. As pain produces or elicits fortitude and endurance; difficulty, perseverance; poverty, industry and ingenuity; danger, courage and what not; so the very virtues, on the other hand, will generate some vices; and, in fine, Mrs. Pendennis had that vice which Miss Pybus and Miss Pierce discovered in her, namely, that of pride; which did not vest itself so much in her own person, as in that of her family.　　2

This pride, and her lamentable softness towards her son make of him a creature incapable of controlling his impulses or of seeing himself in his true light, as the son of a country apothecary, heir to no more than £500 a year and a country estate, with a live-stock of 'nine hens and a cock, a pig, and an old pointer'. More serious is the selfishness and possessiveness which is bound up in her love. Laura perceives that this would have set Helen against her had she and Pen married after his first proposal. It comes out most strongly in the central incident of the novel when her arrival in her son's chambers during his illness leads to the cruel expulsion of Fanny Bolton and the violation of his privacy by the opening of her letter to Pen.

Some readers have fallen into the mistake of thinking that Thackeray approved of this trait in Helen's character, or that, at the least, he failed to realise himself the full cruelty of her be-haviour. This mistake stems from a failure to appreciate the extent to which Thackeray wanted to stress the mixture of motivation and the interpenetration of virtue and vice in the human character. The creator of Helen Pendennis was fully aware of the element of selfishness in her maternal love and of the amount of purely sexual jealousy which is revealed in the behaviour of both Helen and Laura towards Fanny Bolton.

Basic to Thackeray's presentation of these two 'virtuous' women is the idea which he expressed in Chapter 2: 'That even a woman should be faultless . . . is an arrangement not permitted by nature, which assigns to us mental defects . . . without which the scheme of the world could not be carried on.' Selfishness, pride, vanity are essential elements in human nature as Thackeray presents it. The assumptions which underlie *Pendennis* are those which were involved in *Vanity Fair*—that life contains a fundamental mixture of good and evil and a fundamental antagonism between the real and the ideal.

THE HERO!

These are truths which are only realised as such by the hero after a long and painful process of initiation. The novel begins with Pen's first rude awakening into reality, which comes to him when he is thwarted in his impulsive desire to wed Emily Costigan. This is a hard blow, but it is a necessary one if Pen is to realise the nature of the world around him and to distinguish it from the world which he has created and peopled for himself with the enthusiasm and ardour of youth. Yet this first trial carries its danger, which is that from assuming that the world is fresh and virtuous, he will pass in reaction to thinking that it is stale and vicious, or that he will exchange his immature sentimentality for equally immature but more dangerous cynicism. There is little danger that Pen will become like the Major because his initial sensitivity is greater and because he easily perceives that the Major's God is not a god at all. But it is possible that Pen may become something worse, escaping the Major's devotion to a false god only by adopting emotional detachment and a materialism which is frigid where his uncle's is warm. What Pen should learn from the 'Fotheringay' incident when he finally understands that the woman he had worshipped was very ordinary, uncultivated and dull, is that he had misdirected love towards an object which was not worth it. What he tends to do is to assume that there is no object worthy of such love, and that his mistake was a more superficial one than it was in fact. Under the guidance of the Major and impelled by his disappointment at the university, where he fails to graduate, Pen moves towards this cynical position. He prepares to sell himself for a dowry of £10,000 and a seat in Parliament and marry Blanche Amory. What saves him is the example of his mother and Laura. Although they are not perfect, they are a constant reminder that human nature contains the possibility of good as well as the certainty of evil.

At a crucial point in Pen's career his friend Warrington is also an example to him. Warrington is strong in the very ways in which Pen is weak. Pen finds it difficult to set aside his vanity and selfishness and see the world truly, not as the abode of angels or devils but of erring human beings, capable of love. Warrington has firmness of character and clearness of vision, which make him attractive to Laura at the time when she thinks that Pen has compromised himself with Fanny Bolton and lost the essentially youthful enthusiasm and purity of mind which was his principal attraction. But in the final analysis Warrington is deficient in a quality which Pen does possess. By his early marriage he has been prevented from taking an active part and is forced to regard life from the point of view of an onlooker. Even at his worst Pen retains, somewhere in himself, the capacity for involvement in life and the ability to devote himself to a worthwhile cause or person, and this is joined to a purity of heart which saves him in the affair with Fanny Bolton.

Thackeray's intentions in this incident have been misunderstood. In his Preface to the second volume of the first book edition he said:

> Even the gentlemen of our age—this is an attempt to describe one of them, no better nor worse than most educated men—even these we cannot show as they are, with the notorious foibles and selfishness of their lives and their education. Since the author of 'Tom Jones' was buried, no writer of fiction among us has been permitted to depict to his utmost power a MAN. We must drape him, and give him a certain conventional simper. Society will not tolerate the Natural in our Art. Many ladies have remonstrated and subscribers left me, because, in the course of the story, I described a young man resisting and affected by temptation. My object was to say, that he had the passions to feel, and the manliness and generosity to overcome them.

You will not hear—it is best to know it—what moves in the real world, what passes in society, in the clubs, colleges, mess-rooms,— what is the life and talk of your sons. A little more frankness than is customary has been attempted in this story; with no bad desire on the writer's part, it is hoped, and with no ill consequence to any reader.                                                    PREFACE TO VOLUME 2

This passage has been taken as suggesting that Thackeray wished to suggest or would have liked to portray a relationship which proceeded to actual consummation. It is quite clear, however, both here and in the novel itself, that Thackeray did not want us to think that Pen succumbed to the temptation or that he (the author) would have liked to show him succumbing to it. The whole point of Pen's successful resistance to the temptation to seduce a helpless girl of the lower classes is that his character contains a deeply embedded distaste for sexual impurity. An author as interested as Thackeray in the ambiguity of human nature must sometimes have felt the limitations imposed on him by Victorian reading habits and inhibitions. Keenly aware of the existence of those areas of the human mind which are most brilliantly realised in James Joyce's *Ulysses* and of the corrupting influence of Victorian social stratification and modes of education, he must have felt the restrictions imposed on him. On the other hand, it is easy for the modern reader to misunderstand the extent of the freedom for which Thackeray was asking and to forget that he acquiesced in a great number of the limitations imposed on writers, which he felt were to the benefit of society in general.

### THE STRUCTURE OF 'PENDENNIS'

In October 1849 the publication of *Pendennis* was interrupted for three months by an illness which nearly ended fatally. When he fell ill Thackeray had only written the first eleven numbers (Chapters 1–36). It has been asserted that the interval of three months which passed before he wrote the next number brought about a lack of continuity which harmed the structure of the novel. Many critics have asserted that the novel falls into two sections, the first more interesting than the second, and they have argued that it was the interruption of the process of composition which brought this about, preventing the novel from developing as it would otherwise have done. Thackeray did feel rather strange when he began to write again after his illness and thought that certain numbers in the middle of the novel were dull. But on this evidence it has been suggested that the development of the Amory/Altamont plot which takes place after Chapter 36 would not have taken place to the extent now evident had the author not been ill.

This is a difficult argument to defend. If we did not have precise information about the interruption of composition we could not be quite so decided about the point at which the story begins to deteriorate. The structure of the novel as it now stands represents more or less the idea which Thackeray had formed early on. He had some doubts about the way in which the novel should begin and he speaks in his letters about two possible beginnings, a sentimental and a satirical one, but he made up his mind when he heard from a friend the story which is represented in the Amory/Altamont plot. It is worth pointing out that Thackeray introduces Altamont as early as Chapter 26 and that he makes no attempt whatsoever to weave more mystery round the matter of his identity than the most simple-minded novel reader could penetrate at a glance. There are weaknesses in *Pendennis* which prevented the novel from having quite the success enjoyed by *Vanity Fair* and *Esmond*, but they were not caused simply by Thackeray's loss of interest or change of intention.

On the contrary, the part of the story which deals with the Claverings, Altamont and Strong is an integral part of the novel's unity. It is intricately bound up with the story of Pen himself in terms of action and character inter-relation and it relates to the central matter of the hero's development. The part of Blanche Amory, who cannot feel real emotions but must fabricate a personality for herself and falsify the external world in order to obtain the constant emotional stimulus which she needs, is important. The revelation of her character is the last element in Pen's painful progress towards enlightenment and adjustment. The scene between Pen, Blanche and Foker is the deciding factor in the struggle of the hero to throw off a tendency to pose (this time as the martyr to principle). In his relationship with Blanche he comes into significant contrast with Foker, whose career is the reverse to Pen's, taking him from worldly wisdom to worship of the ideal, but with the same sad adjustment to reality at the end of it. This inverse relationship between the careers of the two young men underlines the need for a proper direction of enthusiasm rather than a rejection of it.

Each one of the characters in the group around the Claverings stands in a meaningful relationship to Pen and the problems which he has to overcome. On a simple level, Lady Clavering and Sir Francis relate to the central opposition between selfishness and feeling for others. They are also important because the situation in which they are involved and which grows out of the unintentionally bigamous marriage of Lady Clavering and Sir Francis provides a dramatic commentary on the values of the more central characters, Pen, the Major and Helen Pendennis. The dramatic possibilities of this situation are fully realised, but Thackeray does not attempt to make sensation or melodrama out of it. Far from being interested in excitement, adventure and suspense, he goes out of his way at the end of the novel to stress the comic elements in Altamont's escape and to deflate any other expectations which the reader might have formed. He had originally intended to have Altamont executed at the end of the story; the fact that he changed his mind emphasises the essentially comic nature of the situation which he brings about. Instead of ending on the scaffold, Altamont takes part in a burlesque drama, with the totally unserious Captain Costigan playing second lead, armed with a broomstick—and his story takes second place in a letter primarily devoted to details of the trade in ham and sherry. Altamont scampers out of the story a comic figure, while the Chevalier Strong subsides into refined grocery, nearly resembling the Chevalier Mirobolant, cook to the Claverings.

In sharp contrast to these figures is the valet Morgan, who suddenly emerges from the near anonymity of his service with Major Pendennis to the full status of a villain. Morgan is essentially a more serious villain than Altamont because he has been produced not by chance adventures in foreign lands but by the evils of selfishness and social stratification very near to home. Morgan is a product of the Major's selfishness and the corruptness of the upper classes, whose careless self-concern makes it possible for him to thrive and to become dangerous.

Lady Clavering and Sir Francis are victims to both Altamont and Morgan but their victimisation is financial. Their real unhappiness stems from the materialistic marriage which they contracted, the type of marriage which the Major thought of as the ideal for a sensible man and which Pen and Blanche nearly entered into as well. Altamont and Morgan, in their different ways, provide striking comment on the social situation in which such a marriage can be accepted and approved. Altamont, ex-convict, forger and first husband of Lady Clavering, disguised as a shabby buck, is almost the ghost of her disreputable past, his very existence an attack on the social position for which she was unsuited. Morgan, a living representative of the hollowness of society and the emptiness of its forms, which involve no relationship apart from a financial one, is the perverted 'detective' who brings the affair to light. Ironically he is the bringer of truth!

The Altamont/Clavering plot could have been suitably dealt with on its own, separately from the story of Pen's growth to maturity; and if it had been so treated it would have formed a story of similar proportions to some of Thackeray's early tales, like *A Shabby Genteel Story*. Pen's story could also stand alone. While the two stories are cleverly inter-related in terms of action, and while the Amory/Altamont plot throws light on the central matter, the line of character development on which the novel is most basically constructed is barely affected by the sub-plot. In *David Copperfield* and *Great Expectations*, both of which are concerned with the growth of the central character, a young man not unlike Pen, there is a sense of time which is lacking in *Pendennis*, and an impression of unity which Thackeray's novel does not give. In the early part of the novel the reader is satisfied with the relationship between the pattern of events and the pattern of moral development, but once Pen gets to London and settles down to the literary life our sense of his progression gradually fades. The pattern of events proceeds and in some cases it is directly related to the (as it were) vertical line of Pen's growth, but by no means always. The stream of the novel slows down and spreads out, the drama of tension within the hero is exchanged for the drama of the sub-plot, and when Pen eventually arrives at maturity there is none of the *sense* of arrival, of moral climax, which Dickens succeeded in obtaining.

The train of events which Thackeray began with really peters out with the death of Helen Pendennis, by which time Pen has, to all intents and purposes, announced his allegiance and settled the debate within himself between cynical self-indulgence and purposeful (loving) activity. After Helen's death the focus is shifted from inside the hero to outside, to the antics of Altamont and Chevalier Strong, to incidents like the reconciliation between Fanny Huxter and her husband and his father. We remain interested in all the characters to the end of the novel and we feel a sense of climax in the scene which concludes with Foker's rejection of Blanche and Lady Clavering's discovery that her marriage with Altamont was void. Furthermore, we are aware that basically the same moral statement is involved in the sub-plot and the main plot, and that the assumption that materialism brings unhappiness, while steadfast and clear-sighted love leads to happiness, runs throughout the novel in all its parts. But in the last analysis the novel is defective, a decline from the achievement represented by *Vanity Fair*.

*Pendennis* was a popular novel during and after Thackeray's life. While it presents the world in moral terms it also analyses the Victorian situation in intellectual terms and attempts to resolve the two. Behind the novel there is a discomfort about the relationship between the ideal of what the world should be and the reality of what it is, a tendency to think of growth in terms of progressive corruption, and an idea of adult life as a mode of compromise, all of which were common elements of thought during the period when it was written. But for the modern reader *Pendennis* lacks the interest that *Vanity Fair* has because it is weaker as a novel—partly as an inevitable result of the scheme on which it was constructed. The modern reader, not absorbed in the topicality of the subject, feels that the novel lacks *direction*. It is a coherent whole, each part relating to all other parts in terms of incident and character relationship, and in terms of the general moral design. But the parts do not relate closely enough. Thackeray himself felt this and said in his Preface:

> If this kind of composition, of which the two years' product is now laid before the public, fail in art, as it constantly does and must, it at least has the advantage of a certain truth and honesty, which a work more elaborate might lose. PREFACE TO VOLUME 2

Before he finished *Pendennis* he determined that his next work should be an attempt to reconcile that 'certain truth and honesty' with 'art' and form.

# 6

# Historical Romance

Three months after finishing *Pendennis* Thackeray was a long way towards finishing his next major project, on the success of which he counted to achieve financial security and to replace the fortune which had been lost in his youth. This project resulted in his three lectures, *On the English Humorists of the Eighteenth Century*, which he successfully delivered in some of the major cities in Great Britain before taking them to America in October 1852, where he earned £2,500 in six months. His success with this series encouraged him to embark on another within two years after his return, and his second tour in America, with *The Four Georges*, between October 1855 and April 1856 brought him a further sum of £3,000. The interest in history which resulted in these lectures also led him to write *The History of Henry Esmond*, which is set in the period from 1690 to 1715, and combined with a new interest in America and the relations between the former colonies and England to turn him towards the subject-matter of *The Virginians*.

The period during which the lectures were delivered and *Esmond* was written was not a happy one for Thackeray. Several factors combined to deepen the mood of melancholy and turn his thoughts more closely towards the area of experience which he had already exploited to create Helen Pendennis, with her suffocating love and destructive jealousy. With fame and financial success Thackeray became more isolated from certain of his acquaintances in the London literary world. His straightforward description of the literary life in *Pendennis* forced him into a quarrel with those of his colleagues who were trying to assert the respectability and dignity of the literary profession, and his increasing lack of concern with immediate political and social reform helped to undermine his precarious friendship with Charles Dickens and to prepare for the savage quarrel in which they were later involved. In December 1851, annoyed by a cartoon directed against Napoleon III which he felt was irresponsibly provocative, he finally broke off his connection with *Punch*, leaving himself independent of any commitment to a group or literary organ, though still extremely sensitive to the many attacks which were to be made on his personality and his work.

Meanwhile events in his personal life were causing him an increasing degree of pain. His relationship with his mother—as in disputes over the education of his daughters—was becoming more difficult with her advancing age; and Thackeray became increasingly dissatisfied with the possessive nature of her love for him and the heavy demands which she made on his patience and affection. He wrote to Kate Perry in 1855 with a mixture of patience and bitterness:

> The dear old soul made me pass thirty miserable hours, and kept me awake a night and gave me a headache—What, won't this otherwise saint of a woman ever cease to stab and wound me? . . . . When you are married, when you have a beautiful only son, when you are a widow, why then, take care and don't marry again—for you can't hold the son & the husband too; & from wishing to have too much love at a time, you may lose what once was secure.
>
> Letter to Kate Perry, 19 July 1855

Four years earlier he had revealed the extent of his disillusionment to another female friend, Jane Brookfield:

> A story with a moral. Last night I went to a party at the house of my mother's friend . . . and coming downstairs with my Ma I thought to myself I'll go home and have an hour's chat with her, and try and cheer and console her, for her sad tragic looks melted my heart and always make me think I am a cruel monster: and so I was very tender & sentimental and, you see, caressed her filially as we went down. . . .
>
> But there entered at the house-door a fiddler with his fiddle under his arm: whom when the dear old Mater Dolorosa beheld she said 'O that is M un tel who has come to play a duo with Laure.

I must go back & hear him,' and back she went, and all my sentimentality was gulped down: and I came home. . . .

Letter to Jane Brookfield, 31 January 1851

The disillusionment Thackeray suffered during this period
was more important because he had begun to feel more deeply
than before the loneliness which resulted from the loss of his
wife, still alive and physically sound but incurably insane. In his
loneliness Thackeray turned to Jane Brookfield herself for
consolation, companionship and affection. He had other female
friends, amongst them Kate Perry and Mrs. Proctor, but his
relationship with Jane Brookfield during these years was the
most important that he had. She was the wife of a man whom he
had known at Cambridge. Thackeray had met her as early as
1842 although he did not become intimate with her until they
passed some time together at the country house of mutual friends
in 1848. From that time they seem to have shared their troubles
with each other, she helping him to bear loneliness and he com-
pensating for the formal coldness of her husband. As time went
on, Thackeray became a daily visitor at the Brookfields' London
house. Their friendship was not without its difficulties.
Brookfield himself, though fond of Thackeray, objected to the
intimacy of the relationship and to the tactlessness which
Thackeray showed in making his affection public. In September
1851 the inevitable happened, and Brookfield insisted that Jane
should break off the relationship with Thackeray. She agreed to
do so and gave him his dismissal. Thackeray took it as a terribly
severe deprivation and a hypocritical betrayal, convinced that
Jane loved him more deeply than she loved her husband and was
impelled by weakness or by a cold regard for an empty duty.
When he went to America he made many new friends and
consoled himself by means of playful and restrained flirtation
with several of the young ladies among them. He recovered
from the emotional shock which the rejection had given him
and became able to think of the relationship objectively; but he
remained bitter about it, and the experience with Jane helped to
increase his tendency to analyse affection and to dissect the
female character and the nature of human relations in general.

93

After finishing *Pendennis* Thackeray was also worried by another problem which has often concerned novelists. He felt that with *Vanity Fair* and *Pendennis* he had said all that he had to say, that he lacked fertility and inventiveness. He started at this time to speak of himself as a worn-out volcano and to compare himself unfavourably with other writers in this respect. He wrote to his mother in 1853:

> One of Dickens's immense superiorities over me is the great fecundity of his imagination. He has written 10 books and lo, I am worn out after two. Perhaps Bulwer is better than both of us in this quality. His last book written at 50 is fresher & richer than any he has done. If I last so long: I daresay I shall be busy in Parliamentary Reports: or Historical Studies more possibly at that age. And the drawing, what has become of the drawing?—So, one by one, the flowers of one's youth fade away.
>
> Letter to his Mother, 18 July 1853

To some extent his fears were a result of the ill health which, in his maturity, was rarely absent, and the increasing fatigue which resulted from lecturing and writing under pressure. Certainly they wore away towards the end of his life, though there remained a feeling that he was too old to be dealing with the lighter and more romantic aspects of his story material. But at this time his fears about the possibility of 'drying up' were responsible for the increasing interest in public and political affairs which led him to canvass his aristocratic friends in the hope of obtaining a government place, to keep up his legal connections in order to qualify for a magistracy, and to stand as a candidate in the Oxford by-election of 1857.

Most important of all the effects wrought by Thackeray's increasing concern about his lack of fertility was the interest which he took in historical studies. He had always been interested in history, and especially in the history of the 18th century, and he emphasised this aspect of his career by bringing his early hero, Barry Lyndon, into *The Virginians*, thus connecting his first historical study with his last finished historical novel. Originally his interest may have been stimulated by his reading of Walter

Scott or Thomas Carlyle, who saw European history in terms of recurrent cycles of destruction and regeneration. Thackeray's analysis of the relationship between the 18th century and the 19th is different from Carlyle's in many points but it shows a tendency to contrast the formality and levity of the earlier period with the sincerity and earnestness of the later, which may have been influenced by the terms of reference which Carlyle established in *Sartor Resartus* and the *French Revolution*. He differed from Carlyle in looking at European history as a steady material and social advance which led to an improvement of moral conditions even if it did not affect human nature. In Thackeray's presentation of English history from the beginning of the 18th century he maintains (partly by means of his intrusive narrator and the sense of continuity which he creates) a feeling of tension between the improvement of social conditions and the incorrigible selfishness of the human heart.

Thackeray probably owed as much to Walter Scott as he owed to Carlyle, whose own estimate of Scott was very low. From Scott Thackeray inherited the sense of romance involved with the story of the Stuarts and he added to this his own estimate of the shallowness, selfishness and moral shoddiness of the Hanoverian line. On the other hand, he was also influenced by the *History of England from the Accession of James II*, by Thomas Babington Macaulay. This work, published in separate parts between 1849 and 1861, presented an uncompromisingly Whig and Protestant interpretation of the period up to the death of William III. Thackeray hoped to continue it himself through the reign of Queen Anne, postponing the project several times but always intending to begin it. Macaulay's insistence on the value of freedom from the Stuart autocratic methods of Government and the imposition of Catholicism is reflected in Thackeray's statement that the main value of the Hanoverians was that they left England to govern herself. He did not lose his interest in the Stuarts, with their ability to attract romantic and enthusiastic loyalty, but the picture of them which he presents shows them in basic opposition to the interests of the country and lacking those very qualities of self-control, determination and

earnestness of purpose which, in the person of his central characters in both *Esmond* and *The Virginians*, he puts forward as most
estimable.

After his disappointment with *Pendennis* Thackeray attempted to
make his next novel as near to formal perfection as he could.
He decided not to publish it in numbers, as he had published his
previous full-length novels, but to give himself the time to
shape it as a whole before publication. Even so, he was not
completely satisfied with it. He had determined at an early
stage that the novel was to have 'some very good lofty and
generous people', probably thinking of it in part as a reply to the
accusations of meanness and sordidness which had been thrown
at him on account of *Vanity Fair* and *Pendennis*. But as the novel
went on he began to express some concern about the tone of
melancholy which pervaded it. Before the novel was finished
he wrote to his mother:

> I wish the new novel wasn't so grand and melancholy—the hero is
> as stately as Sir Charles Grandison—something like Warrington—a
> handsome likeness of an ugly son of yours—There's a deal of pains
> in it. . . .           Letter to his Mother, 17–18 November 1851

Later, when he had finished the first volume, he was more pleased
with it, thinking that the story grew more lively as it proceeded,
but shortly after it was published he wrote to a friend:

> . . . my book just out is as dreary and dull as if it were true: the
> Author was not very cheerful when he wrote it.
>                         Letter to Lady Pollock, 27 October 1852

These comments should not be taken too seriously as indicating
a genuine dissatisfaction with the novel. In Thackeray's reaction
to reviews of *Esmond* and in his comments about its reception
one can see a considerable amount of satisfaction. *The Times*
came out with an adverse criticism, attacking the historical
novel in general and *Esmond* in particular because it presented a
gloomy picture of human nature and showed an incapacity to
conceive of 'human perfection'. Thackeray's comment on this

review in a letter to his daughter Harriet indicates his confidence in his own conception:

> I was pleased—The man cannot understand what I am writing any more than poor Jack Forster; and it's quite as right that they should speak and think ill of my writing, as that I should continue on my own way.          Letter to Harriet Thackeray, 17 January 1853

Later, in *The Virginians*, he made a statement which shows that he was trying to do with the historical novel something which had not been done before. Not long before he wrote *Esmond* he had written *Rebecca and Rowena* (1850), and attacked the romantic or idealised concept of history. In *The Virginians* he further clarified his attitude by warning the readers that his version of history had nothing in common with that of Thomas Carlyle. Referring to the latter's *History of Frederick the Great*, which was at that time being published, he said:

> Would you have this history compete with yonder book? Could my jaunty yellow park-phaeton run counter to that grim chariot of thundering war? Could my meek little jog-trot Pegasus meet the shock of yon steed of foaming bit and flaming nostril? Dear kind reader (with whom I love to talk from time to time, stepping down from the stage where our figures are performing, attired in the habits and using the parlance of past ages),—my kind patient reader! it is a mercy for both of us that Harry Warrington did not follow the King of the Borussians, as he was minded to do, for then I should have had to describe battles which Carlyle is going to paint: and I don't wish you should make odious comparisons between me and that master.                    THE VIRGINIANS 62

Stripped of its modesty and taken in conjunction with Thackeray's comment that *Esmond* was dreary enough to be true, this passage amounts to a warning to the reader that it is not the intention of the author to provide excitement by describing external events but that he is concerned, on the contrary, to undermine the concept of the heroic and the exciting.

This is what he does in *Esmond*. The novel is based on a contrast between the mundane domestic virtues and emotions and the more stimulating concepts of idealised love and heroic behaviour.

Of all the characters in the novel, Father Holt, the Duke of Marlborough and Beatrix Esmond, all in different ways, approach most nearly to the heroic ideal. Holt captures the imagination of the youthful Henry Esmond:

> ... his delight in their walks was to tell Harry of the glories of his order, of its martyrs and heroes, of its Brethren converting the heathen by myriads, traversing the desert, facing the stake, ruling the courts and councils, or braving the tortures of kings; so that Harry Esmond thought that to belong to the Jesuits was the greatest prize of life and bravest end of ambition; the greatest career here and in heaven the surest reward. ESMOND I, 3

As Harry grows older, freed from the influence of Holt, he learns to see the Jesuit in a clear light, and by the time that he meets him again in Flanders Holt has dwindled to the size of a very fallible if persistent conspirator. Our last glimpse of him, in the crowd gathered to welcome George I to England, reveals him in the strongest light of day as a comic figure.

In his treatment of the Duke of Marlborough Thackeray takes full account of the great general's heroic and martial qualities but insists on the enormous selfishness which led the Duke from one treason to another and which was, in fact, at the root of his success. War is treated as in *Barry Lyndon*, its glamour removed and its sordidness and brutality stressed by Henry Esmond, who devotes himself to it from a sense of duty rather than a desire for glory. Esmond makes it quite clear that Marlborough's astounding success is partly due to his equally astounding inability to feel for himself or for others:

> Our chief, whom England and all Europe, saving only the Frenchmen, worshipped almost, had this of the godlike in him, that he was impassable before victory, before danger, before defeat. Before the greatest obstacle or the most trivial ceremony; before a hundred thousand men drawn in battalia, or a peasant slaughtered at the door of his burning hovel; before a carouse of drunken German lords, or a monarch's court, or a cottage table where his plans were laid, or an enemy's battery, vomiting flame and death, and strewing corpses round about him; he was always cold, calm, resolute, like fate. ESMOND II, 9

His ally and rival, Prince Eugene of Savoy, was impelled by anger and hatred against the French King, becoming in time of battle 'possessed by a sort of warlike fury'. Marlborough was never involved or disturbed:

> Our Duke was as calm at the mouth of the cannon as at the door of a drawing-room. Perhaps he could not have been the great man he was, had he had a heart either for love or hatred, or pity or fear, or regret or remorse. ESMOND II, 9

Beatrix Esmond shares this quality. She is totally removed from those around her, drawn into emotional involvement only on the rarest occasions. It is disappointed ambition which strikes her most deeply when the Duke of Hamilton is killed and her marriage prevented, and she responds to it in heroic fashion. Esmond reports:

> Whatever her feelings might have been of anger or of sorrow (and I fear me that the former emotion was that which most tore her heart), she would take no confidant, as people of softer natures would have done under such a calamity; her mother and her kinsman knew that she would disdain their pity, and that to offer it would be but to infuriate the cruel wound which fortune had inflicted.
> ESMOND III, 7

Esmond does not condemn this inhuman selfishness but rather treats is as the law of a certain kind of nature, opposed to the nature of those who can feel:

> Friends and children of our race, who come after me, in which way will you bear your trials? I know one that prays God will give you love rather than pride, and that the Eye all-seeing shall find you in the humble place. Not that we should judge proud spirits otherwise than charitably. 'Tis nature hath fashioned some for ambition and dominion, as it hath formed others for obedience and gentle submission. The leopard follows her nature as the lamb does, and acts after leopard law; she can neither help her beauty, nor her courage, nor her cruelty; nor a single spot on her shining coat; nor the conquering spirit which impels her; nor the shot which brings her down. ESMOND III, 7

99

The ability to give and to receive love is not presented in such a simple way in *Esmond* as it is in Thackeray's early work. In both *Vanity Fair* and *Pendennis*, by means of Amelia and Helen Pendennis, Thackeray stressed the destructive potentiality of emotionalism. In creating Rachel, Lady Castlewood, Thackeray achieved his most complex and moving embodiment of the concept of feeling unqualified by a controlling consciousness and sense of balance. The relationship between Rachel and Henry Esmond was a source of deep offence to many contemporary readers, who complained that their marriage was like that of a mother with a son. The strength of Victorian reaction against the situation which Thackeray described is a measure of its accuracy and complexity. Believing (well before Freud) that sexual jealousy was an element in maternal relationships, Thackeray describes that between Rachel and Henry as expanding beyond the proscribed limits under the impulse of sexual attraction. As Thackeray describes it, their relationship is never properly that of a mother and a son, Rachel responding to Henry in sexual terms right from the start, though she is unaware of it. Awareness is forced on her by the intensity of the passion which she feels for him, and her unwillingness to admit it for what it is makes her repress it and act outrageously in the affair of Harry's visit to the blacksmith's daughter. Self-knowledge comes to her eventually after the duel in which her husband is killed and Harry wounded. The violence of her emotion frightens her and she transmutes it into anger against Harry for being involved in the affair in which the husband towards whom she feels guilty is killed. Her anger brings him to despair, he strikes his wounded arm against the wall and falls unconscious. Before he regains consciousness Rachel steals a button from the sleeve of his coat, and it is only at the very end of the story that we hear of this button again. We are not given the information about it before the end because Harry himself did not know what had become of it. When he reminds us of it at the end of the memoir it amounts to his telling us that he has discovered the extent and duration of Rachel's love and that the understanding between them is complete.

The reader (and there has been such) who objects to the marriage of Rachel and Henry on the grounds that he takes her as a kind of second best misses the central point of *Esmond*. The marriage with Rachel is accompanied by Henry's withdrawal from Europe. Both acts are committed in a mood of disappointment, but what Thackeray wishes us to understand by the end of the novel is not that Henry is putting up with a second best but that he is reconciling himself to life as it is. The story of Henry and Rachel is played against a background of European events and in a period when emotional involvement and the attainment of an ideal are irreconcilable. Henry's last chance of obtaining Beatrix rests on the success of his plot to restore the Stuarts, and fails because of the character of the Pretender. At the end of the story Henry has learnt that the restoration of the Stuarts, to whom alone emotional commitment is possible, would not be in the interests of the country, and that the Hanoverian cause, which would serve the country, is one to which he could commit himself only on grounds of selfish materialism. Henry's last involvement in public affairs amounts to a playing out of those childish aspirations towards the heroic ideal which he had kept since his childhood. His final turning away from Beatrix occurs when he realises that she, who represents the ideal of beauty for him, demanding heroic service, is inexorably attracted to the empty form of royalty, the mere simulacrum of chivalric attainment.

The world which Beatrix wants, and in which her qualities are most actively operative, is the world of Marlborough and of Mohun. Mohun, who kills both Beatrix's father and her intended husband, the Duke of Hamilton, is able to operate only by exploiting the code of formal chivalry and honour to which Beatrix also gives her allegiance. He is presented throughout the story as a character with the same basically unfeeling nature as Beatrix and Marlborough, a leopard rather than a lamb, an animal the law of whose nature is to kill. Esmond rejects the world in which such principles are operative and withdraws from a life in which he had earlier striven to attain. His later years in America are not unmarked by a mood of melancholy which pervades his memoir. His biography is that of a man who has failed and ceased to strive because he knows that the object for which he had striven is worthless and that the act of striving is no longer possible for the unselfish man. What he accepts instead is not faultless or ideal in any way—the character of Rachel Esmond is heavily marked by the jealousy which his daughter's preface tells us continued into later life. But what Esmond achieves is above all real and valuable beyond all those things which he rejects. Esmond has failed in his search for an impossible and empty ideal and perhaps fallen short in his attempt to obtain 'earthly joy' but he has attained to the summit of earthly happiness, to the real love of his wife:

> As I think of the immense happiness which was in store for me, and of the depth and intensity of that love which, for so many years, hath blessed me, I own to a transport of wonder and gratitude for such a boon—nay, am thankful to have been endowed with a heart capable of feeling and knowing the immense beauty and value of the gift which God hath bestowed upon me. Sure, love *vincit omnia*; is immeasurably above all ambition, more precious than wealth, more noble than name. He knows not life who knows not that: he hath not felt the highest faculty of the soul who hath not enjoyed it. In the name of my wife I write the completion of hope, and the summit of happiness. To have such a love is the one blessing, in comparison of which all earthly joy is of no value; and to think of her, is to praise God. ESMOND III, 13

'THE VIRGINIANS'

Thackeray did not write *The Virginians* immediately after *Esmond*; *The Newcomes* intervened; but the two novels belong together in so far as the later novel is a continuation of the earlier one, suggested by the Preface in which the daughter of Rachel and Henry Esmond is introduced. Thackeray originally wrote this Preface in order to suggest a point of view other than that of the narrator and to qualify Henry's enthusiasm about his later life. His letters and journals give no indication of the time when he first thought of *The Virginians*, but during the visits to America in 1852 and 1855 he collected material for the novel and began it as soon as he returned from the second tour in May 1856. It was published in numbers between November 1857 and November 1859.

The scope of *The Virginians* is much wider than that of its predecessor. By means of the intrusive narrator Thackeray made explicit the comparison between the 18th century and the 19th which was implicit in *Esmond*, and he also made an extended comparison between America and England, again using his narrator to stress the fact that logical right or wrong is to be considered apart from the moral nature of the societies involved in political conflict. At the same time he was following through from *Esmond* the families and individuals involved in that novel in order to expand or to qualify the statements which he had already made.

To a certain extent these intentions seem to have conflicted and to have combined with the method of publication to deprive the novel of that formal unity and simplicity which *Esmond* possessed and for which it has always been praised. *The Virginians* is most successful in treating the characters who are involved in the action of *Esmond* or who descend from other characters who were, and least successful in relating to this part of the novel the statement involved in the conflict between the two countries (see pp. 106–7). Beatrix Esmond appears in the later novel at an advanced age, having lived according to the plan which she outlined for herself in *Esmond*. Hinting only at the scenes of sordidness and debauchery through which she has passed, Thackeray presents her as drained of all but the most superficial emotions and yet momentarily restored to human nature by the conjunction of youth, beauty and resemblance to their grandfather in Harry and George Warrington.

Beatrix has always been considered a successful characterisation, but she is no more vivid than Rachel Esmond Warrington, the mistress of the Virginian estates and a representative of disorganised and selfish emotionalism who spreads pain and mistrust around her, ruined as a friend and mother by the incapacity to examine her own motives and actions—'Feelings were her reasons'. As a result she imposes excruciating pain on those around her and forces her dependants into a life of sordid deceit and selfish scheming which results in Fanny Mountain's exploitation of the openness and innocent emotionalism of Harry Warrington.

Against Beatrix Esmond, Rachel Warrington and the English Esmonds, the head of whom, the Earl of Castlewood, is a brilliant and somehow attractive embodiment of total detachment, Thackeray places the Warrington brothers and the Lambert family, who manage to combine restraint, common sense and sensibility. From them George chooses his bride, Theo, and when they have broken through the barrier of pride which Madame Esmond sets up between them he begins a life centred on the domestic affections.

George, however, fails to obtain complete happiness. After the marriage (at the beginning of Chapter 72) Thackeray makes a radical shift in point of view, putting the editor/narrator in the background and completing the story by means of quoting the memoir which George writes for his family. This has two effects. It gives a further dimension, allowing us to foresee the eventual happiness of the couple and so to concentrate on their reactions to present circumstances rather than on the circumstances themselves, and reduces the element of romance by indicating a very commonplace future and very commonplace children. It also allows Thackeray to enter into the consciousness of George to an extent difficult by other means.

In telling the story of George's life after his marriage, Thackeray wanted to deflate exaggerated ideas of happiness and to investigate the conditions of such happiness as we may expect. Female censorship of the manuscript of George's memoir prevents us from hearing about what Thackeray hints is his disappointment with his wife, but we are allowed to see the extent to which George is in need of some kind of purposeful activity after his inheritance from Sir Miles Warrington. This need is satisfied when he fights in America on the Royalist side, just as Harry's is when he fights for the rebels. This amounts to a rejection of the line of conduct followed by their grandfather, who withdrew from action, rejecting with it the principle of self-seeking as beneath him and that of devotion to a cause as historically inappropriate.

The youthful Harry is attracted to military action out of a naïve desire for glory, but Thackeray does not allow his principles to pass unquestioned. Both Major-General Lambert and General Wolfe become soldiers from the very highest principles, but their motivation is duty rather than glory. The matter is discussed in a conversation between Harry and Wolfe, then a Colonel:

> 'To have such a good name, and to live such a life as Colonel Lambert's,' said Wolfe, 'seem to me now the height of human ambition.'
>
> 'And glory and honour?' asked Warrington. 'Are those nothing? and would you give up the winning of them?'
>
> 'They were my dreams once,' answered the Colonel, who had now different ideas of happiness, 'and now my desires are much more tranquil. I have followed arms ever since I was fourteen years of age. I have seen almost every kind of duty connected with my calling. I know all the garrison towns in this country, and have had the honour to serve wherever there has been work to be done during the last ten years . . . and now, methinks, I would like quiet, books to read, a wife to love me, and some children to dandle on my knee. I have imagined some such Elysium for myself, Mr. Warrington. True love is better than glory; and a tranquil fireside, with the woman of your heart seated by it, the greatest good the gods can send us.'  THE VIRGINIANS 24

It is impossible to take this comment without any qualification because we know that it is influenced by Wolfe's particular situation; but Thackeray is concerned in *The Virginians* to emphasise duty and commitment to a greater extent than he had done in *Esmond*, always balancing the domestic virtues against the active ones and never allowing the reader to forget the essential relativity of human happiness:

> Happy! who is happy? Was there not a serpent in Paradise itself, and if Eve had been perfectly happy beforehand, would she have listened to him?  4

Thackeray made several changes in the plan of this novel even as he was writing it. Originally the incidents of the War of Independence were to have taken up a far greater proportion of the novel than they eventually did. During the process of composition he was concerned over the lack of incident and evidently suffered from his commitment to a plot involving a good deal of action and to a form of publication which placed a premium on stirring incident. He wrote to an American friend as he was trying to write the seventh number:

> The book's clever but stupid thats the fact. I hate story-making incidents, surprises, love-making, &c more and more every day: and here is a third of a great story done equal to two thirds of an ordinary novel—and nothing actually has happened, except that a young gentleman has come from America to England.
>
> Letter to Mrs. Baxter, 10–23 April 1858

To the family of the same friend he complained four months later:

> . . . what a horribly stupid story I am writing! Don't tell me. I know better than any of you. No incident, no character no go left in this dreary old expiring carcass.
>
> Letter to the Baxters, 25 August 1858

To a considerable extent this concern was justified—not because *The Virginians* should necessarily have had more action but because the scheme which Thackeray had suggested in his very first paragraph and which he recurred to at the end of the novel meant that the two brothers should have been seen primarily against the background of the events which resulted from the conflict between England and America. Thackeray was also interested in portraying the two youths in the context of English society, to contrast them by means of its reaction to them and so make an analysis of the social setting. This he could have done and at the same time have retained all that was most valuable in the realisation of English characters and social setting had he chosen to make the contrast between the two men a running contrast. As it was, he was drawn into the trap of treating each young man separately as an inevitable result of wanting to show Harry reacting to prosperity and so having to dispose of George for a considerable time. However, even after the break in continuity which comes with George's return, the novel does not break up. The real point of tension comes with George's marriage and the adoption of his point of view. This might have been necessary to allow Thackeray to stress the impossibility of happiness and to deflate our expectations of domestic bliss but it prevented the balance between George and Harry from being restored and consequently reduced the reader's interest in the contrast between them, on which the unity of the novel depended. *The Virginians* is an interesting novel and contains some brilliant scenes, like the death of Beatrix Esmond, but it shows Thackeray succumbing to the pressure of conflicting claims and losing interest in the direct line of narrative on which it was supposed to be constructed. In contrast, *Esmond* has a simplicity and severity of form, achieved primarily by the use of a fixed point of view, which has made many critics argue that it is Thackeray's most successful novel—not excluding *Vanity Fair*.

# 7

# 'The Newcomes'

The publication of *Esmond* and *The Virginians* was separated by a period of five years, during which Thackeray wrote and published another novel in numbers—*The Newcomes*, which appeared in the yellow jackets which he kept for all his publications of this kind between October 1853 and August 1855. The novel was not begun in a very cheerful mood; by this time Thackeray was becoming increasingly worried about what he felt was his lack of inventiveness and inability to make a story run easily with the element of excitement and incident necessary to serial publication. While he was writing the second number (Chapters 4–6), he wrote to his mother:

> . . . I can't but see it is a repetition of past performances, and think that vein is pretty nigh worked out in me. Never mind: this is not written for glory but for quite as good an object namely money; w^h will profit the children more than reputation. . . .
>
> Letter to his Mother, 18 July 1853

Three weeks later he wrote to a friend:

> I'm in low spirits about the Newcomes. It's not good. It's stupid. It haunts me like a great stupid ghost. I think it says why do you go on writing this rubbish? You are old, you have no more invention &c.
>
> Letter to Sarah Baxter, 7 August 1853

As he got farther into the novel his mood changed. A good part of it was written while he was abroad on holiday with his daughters, and his programme of composition was seriously interrupted by bouts of illness which attacked all the family and by persistent visitations of the complaints from which he habitually suffered. By February 1854, when he had finished the seventh number (Chapters 24–6), the publishers reported that the public were beginning to complain about the lack of incident. By this time, however, Thackeray had begun to feel confident in the quality of the novel and to think in terms of a steady climactic development. He told his mother that he intended to disregard the petitions of the publishers and he wrote to their representative with assurances as to the interest which was about to develop:

> So they have found out that there's no story have they? There is one coming: and I think it will be a very good one. No IX [Chapters 27–9] w^h I have done is a stunning number for incident and there's plenty of action & passion too from that stage of the story to the end of the XXV numbers.
> ... Tell B[radbury] & E[vans] not to lose heart about it I know if I live it will be a very good one. It has a slow beginning to be sure. But just wait. In IX & X [Chapters 30–2] the people are all moving very friskily and in Vol II. there will be some lively business. Let 'em talk. I'm not afraid. . . .
>
> Letter to Percival Leigh, 25 February 1854

After this his opinion of the novel did not change. Maintaining a steady control over the story, he planned each part of the novel in advance and wrote to John Blackwood as early as December 1854 saying that the last six numbers would be the most interesting. Almost two years after he had finished it he came across two numbers while on a lecture tour in Scotland and could not help expressing his satisfaction with them.

The relative slowness of the early chapters of *The Newcomes* was an inevitable result of the design which Thackeray had drawn out for himself. The establishment of the characters, their setting and their history had to precede the account of the several strands of action which take up the later parts of the novel. In *The Newcomes*, as several critics have pointed out, Thackeray is creating a society rather than sketching in a background to a group of characters. In this novel he exploits to a greater degree than before his own tendency to make references to a wide background of biblical history, classical myth and fable. In all

Thackeray's work an erring and aggressive wife tends to appear as Mrs. Potiphar, a brother treated harshly as Joseph, a friend in need as a Good Samaritan. In *The Newcomes* there are more of such references than is usual and their range is wider. A typical example is the sentence with which Thackeray ends a description of the youthful Barnes Newcome: 'In a word, he was as scrupulously whited as any sepulchre in the whole bills of mortality' (Chapter 8). The phrase 'bills of mortality' refers to the parishes in and around central London, the whited sepulchre to *Matthew* 23, xxvii and *Acts* 23, iii. By bringing them together Thackeray neatly combines a timeless moral statement with a contemporary placing which gives the former added point and application. On the title-page of the novel the sub-title, *Memoirs of a most Respectable Family*, is surrounded by a number of pictures representing the various animal fables (see illustrations). The first chapter takes up and expands this reference which recurs in the postscript to the novel. By using it Thackeray borrows from the fable some of the timeless moral applicability which belongs to it and strengthens the tone with which *The Newcomes* is pervaded.

Thackeray's subject in *The Newcomes* is a wide one—nothing less than the social behaviour of human beings. In the early sections of the novel he creates the context in which the particular human action must be seen, spending some time in establishing the reader's sense of time and place. The novel deals with more than one generation and more than one social group. The Newcome family in its gradual rise is employed to give us a full sense of the social stratifications and the relations between them, and we are given a keen sense of the different social values and habits which prevail in other societies in India and France. With the ninth number (Chapters 27–9) we move to Germany for the family Congress of the Newcomes where nearly all the main characters of the novel are brought together to take part in the materialistic intrigue which precedes the solemnisation of marriage in the respectable world. The only two main characters who are absent from this gathering are Colonel Newcome and the Countess de Florac. Their absence is appropriate because neither of them belongs to the group which is gathered at the fashionable resort. The Newcome family is a line stretching from humble origins in the industrial town of Newcome, after which the foundling, Thomas Newcome, is named, to the Marquis of Farintosh and the Duc d'Ivry. Clive's father and the Countess belong only nominally to the group of people involved in the activities of the respectable world and only nominally to the 'respectable' families or to the materialistic world in which they live.

In the very simplest terms *The Newcomes* is based on the opposition between social life and the domestic virtues, as Thackeray's previous work had been. There is a basic contrast between the respectable world and the Bohemian world, the one a place where the natural desires and impulses are forced and stunted, the other an abode of licence and naturalness. There are several characters in the novel who try to reconcile their social interests with what they recognise as a conflicting code of morality—Lord Kew and Jack Belsize are the most sympathetic examples; they try to make the gentlemanly code of behaviour contain both principles. But both Kew and Belsize are forced to make dramatic statements of allegiance. Kew, after the duel into which he is forced by the jealousy of a former mistress, recognises that the pattern of behaviour which society permits and even encourages a young man to follow is evil and tends to the destruction of peace of mind and happiness. Poor Jack, whose herculean struggle to overcome his love for Clara Pulleyn and to serve the code of gentlemanly restraint proves to be beyond the bounds of his endurance, breaks out and acts disastrously. Frederick Bayham, superficially resembling the other two men, his social superiors, belongs to Bohemia, where the individual is free to follow his own impulses at the expense of respectability and morality. The way of life which Thackeray advocates in this novel is neither the social nor the Bohemian; it is a third, in which natural impulses are restricted but trained in their growth by the influence of morality and self-restraint.

The action of the novel begins in Bohemia, the careless disreputable *demi-monde* of 19th-century London where Colonel Newcome takes his son. Newcome responds well to the innocent

aspects of Bohemian life, enjoys the singing and easy comrade-
ship, but reacts forcefully and naïvely to the indecency which is a
normal part of it. That the novel should begin in this way is
important because in this opening scene we have a clear impression of the essential simplicity of the Colonel, an idea of the
relationship between himself and Clive, and are made aware
that the rejection of social values which is to follow does not
involve the acceptance of the more irregular aspects of the life
to which it is normally opposed.

The Colonel is the central figure in the early parts of the novel
and he has our entire sympathy in his gradual realisation of the
difference between the social code of the respectable world and
the more simple one which he brought back from India where
people felt and acted on their feelings and it was relatively easy
to tell good from evil. But it is essential to understand that neither
the Colonel nor any other character is being put forward as a
mouthpiece for the author. One of the main differences between
Thackeray's early work and his later is the enormously greater
subtlety and sensitivity to moral and social complexity which is
shown in the latter. The exaltation of the domestic virtues,
purity of heart and directness of feeling is a basic part of
Thackeray's creed, and Colonel Newcome is the most forceful
and touching example of a man governing his life by such
principles. At the same time, however, as he wished to inculcate
a respect for unselfish feeling, Thackeray was highly aware of its
dangers and of the terrifyingly narrow boundary between love
and hate. This awareness had already been shown in Helen
Pendennis and Lady Castlewood. In *The Newcomes* it is strikingly
dramatised in the person of Thomas Newcome, who becomes
the victim of his own emotions.

THE NARRATOR OF 'THE NEWCOMES' AND THE AUTHOR'S POINT
OF VIEW

Thackeray chose to write *The Newcomes* under the cover of
Arthur Pendennis, to whom the narration is given, so that he
would have freedom to say things which might have been impossible to him in his own person. Doubtless this made him feel

freer to deal with topics as dangerous in the Victorian novel as the elopement of Clara Newcome with Lord Highgate. But more important was the freedom it gave him to put forward a number of attitudes to the situations which he described and to imply a standard of judgment which could not easily have been spoken.

Pendennis admits that he is not omniscient as a narrator:

> ... in the present volumes where dialogues are written down which the reporter could by no possibility have heard, and where motives are detected which the persons actuated by them certainly never confided to the writer, the public must once for all be warned that the author's individual fancy very likely supplies much of the narrative; and that he forms it as best he may out of stray papers, conversations reported to him, and his knowledge, right or wrong, of the characters of the persons engaged. And, as is the case with the most orthodox histories, the writer's own guesses or conjectures are printed in exactly the same type as the most ascertained patent facts.
>
> THE NEWCOMES 24

This passage goes no farther than to suggest that there is a possibility of mistaken or incomplete assessment on the part of the narrator or editor. Later in the novel Pen admits to being at the mercy of conflicting attitudes to the action which he is describing. A few phrases from a speech of Warrington's—'This man goes about his life business ... as a bug that stinks and stings' (Chapter 54)—tell us that he, who echoes the language of Alexander Pope's description of Sporus (Lord Hervey), takes up the position of the traditional satirist, not far from that which Thackeray himself took up in *Men's Wives*. Laura, on the other hand, is the representative of respectable Christianity. Pen is torn between them, not knowing what to think about the actions and characters of whom they both speak. In Chapter 64 he says:

> In the stage which the family feud now reached, and which the biographer of the Newcomes is bound to describe, there is one gentle moralist who gives her sentence decidedly against Clive's father; whilst, on the other hand, a rough philosopher and friend of mine, whose opinions used to have some weight with me, stoutly declares that they were right. 64

Pen's dilemma as a narrator is obviously part of the novel itself. It allowed Thackeray to distance his action and to shift responsibility. It also permitted him to achieve a subtlety of handling of some of the central incidents of the novel that he never surpassed.

One of the most important of these incidents is the elopement of Clara Newcome and Lord Highgate. The skill with which it was handled is indicated by the fact that after a favourable review in *The Times* Charles Mudie, owner of the largest circulating library in Britain and arbiter of taste to the middle-class reader, increased his order for *The Newcomes* by one hundred. Only four years later Mudie's reaction to the frankness of a seduction scene in George Meredith's *The Ordeal of Richard Feverel* caused him to withdraw his order and irretrievably damage the sale of the book. Most Victorian readers would have thought the mere rendering of an incident like the elopement in *The Newcomes* an indication that the author was asserting a woman's right to leave her husband for a lover. Two factors in Thackeray's handling of the incident made this impossible. He brought Laura Pendennis to the foreground with her pious, prudish and sickeningly cruel use of Lady Clara's children to persuade her to stay with Sir Barnes. And he made sure that the elopement was followed by an appropriate degree of unhappiness.

The treatment of this incident cannot be acceptable to the modern reader unless he appreciates the fact that the author dissociates himself from the attitude of Laura. His allegiance to her as a spokesman is not nearly as total as may seem. He told a friend that he did not like her and he replied to a reviewer who criticised her prudery and conceit by saying that he wanted Pen's willingness to be guided by her to indicate his weakness rather than his own sympathy with her point of view. In fact we have attitudes to the elopement which are clearly distinct from hers; notably, that of the Comte de Florac. Furthermore, those who know most of the affairs of a family, as Thackeray frequently reminds us, are the servants, and they stand by Lady Clara, treating her with undiminished respect. Ultimately their loyalty and devotion carry more weight than Laura's condemnation. Society pays Lady Clara back and by the code of feeling which demands a mother's sacrifice for the sake of her children she stands condemned. It was an important part of Thackeray's intention that his readers should realise the distress which the elopement caused, but he wished also to ensure that the incident should not be taken too simply. The manipulation of Pen as narrator ensures the fact that the human elements and the social values, for both of which Thackeray had respect, should be properly balanced and that the effect should be subtle rather than crudely 'Victorian' or irresponsibly 'Bohemian'.

The social and human analysis which produced *The Newcomes* was very keen indeed. Throughout the novel Thackeray reminds us of the essential loneliness of the individual, and shows society substituting empty and meaningless social relationships for those based on feeling and human nature. At the beginning of Chapter 24 the narrator discourses on the essential separateness of human beings:

> One ship crosses another ship, and, after a visit from one captain to his comrade, they sail away each on his course. The *Clive Newcome* meets a vessel which makes signals that she is short of bread and water; and after supplying her, our captain leaves her to see her no more. One or two of the vessels with which we commenced the voyage together, part company in a gale, and founder miserably; others, after being woefully battered in the tempest, make port, or are cast upon surprising islands where all sorts of unlooked-for prosperity await the lucky crew. 24

The incident described in Chapter 19, 'The Colonel at Home', shows the different ways in which people may react to this basic fact of human separateness. Social life tends to increase the distance between individuals, to substitute empty form for real contact. The two sisters-in-law, Clive's aunts, illustrate the breakdown of familial relationships in the social world:

> The sisters-in-law kissed on meeting, with that cordiality so delightful to witness in sisters who dwell together in unity. It was, 'My dear Maria, what an age since I have seen you!' 'My dear Ann, our occupations are so engrossing, our circles are so different,' in a languid response from the other. 19

In contrast, Lord Kew, when called upon by various people to deny his connection with the person who had invited him, and to join them in asserting their essential distinctness, responds with common sense and sincerity:

'. . . I have been in the house only five minutes, and three people have said the same thing to me—Mrs. Newcome, who is sitting downstairs in a rage waiting for her carriage, the condescending Barnes, and yourself. Why do *you* come here, Smee?'    19

Colonel Newcome, too, in following the law of his simple nature, breaks through the barriers between person and person, and comforts the loneliness of the pathetic governess, Miss Quigley:

He behaves with splendid courtesy to Miss Quigley, the governess, and makes a point of taking wine with her, and of making a most profound bow during that ceremony. Miss Quigley cannot help thinking Colonel Newcome's bow very fine. . . . If Ethel makes for her uncle purses, guard-chains, antimacassars, and the like beautiful and useful articles, I believe it is in reality Miss Quigley who does four fifths of the work, as she sits alone in the school room, high, high up in that lone house, when the little ones are long since asleep, before her dismal little tea-tray, and her little desk, containing her mother's letters and her mementoes of home.    20

It is, however, in his relationship with Clive that we see the Colonel struggling most to achieve closeness and unity. Years before, when he lost his Leonore, who was forced to marry the Comte de Florac in fulfilment of her father's empty pledge, he had been forced back into the loneliness which surrounded him in childhood. Away from Clive in India he put all his faith and hope on the possibility of a permanent and unified relationship with his son. In Europe, as Clive grows up, he is compelled to acknowledge that contact as close as he had dreamed of is impossible. Separated from Clive by the very relationship which brought them together, he returns to India so as to allow his son to grow up in his own way. In depicting his disappointment, Thackeray achieves a fine pathos:

So, as he thought what vain egotistical hopes he used to form about the boy when he was away in India—how in his plans for the happy future Clive was to be always at his side; how they were to read, work, play, think, be merry together—a sickening and humiliating sense of the reality came over him, and he sadly contrasted it with the former fond anticipations. Together they were, yet he was alone still.                    21

At this stage in his career the Colonel is entirely sympathetic, though Thackeray shared some of the reservations which the modern reader might have about him. He wrote to his mother while he was in the middle of the eighth number (Chapters 24–6): 'The Colonel is going to India the day after tomorrow. You'll be glad to hear that, I know. He is a dear old boy but confess you think he is rather a twaddler?' (4 January 1854). Later in the novel he begins to change and to lose the reader's sympathy. After his return from India he tries, with increasing desperation, to assert his influence on his son's life. Never understanding Clive's attempts to devote himself to painting, he forces him into a marriage which is against his deeper wishes and succeeds in bringing about a situation which his own marital experience should have taught him to avoid. Ironically, the Colonel's own loneliness makes him marry Clive to a wife totally unsuitable for him and so emphasise his son's separation from the woman he really loved. At the same time the Colonel allows his frustration over the loss of communication between himself and his son to colour his attitude to other people and drive him into a bitter and reasonless feud with Sir Barnes Newcome. His frantic desire to control his son's destiny and to enable him to marry Ethel had led him to enter the Bundlecund Banking Company, which to some extent was an unselfish action. As the novel proceeds, however, the Colonel begins to suffer from the vice of self-esteem, losing his humility and modesty together with his sense of proportion. He becomes, as it were, materialistic by proxy:

Now this Bundlecund Banking Company, in the Colonel's eyes, was in reality his son Clive. But for Clive there might have been a hundred banking companies established, yielding a hundred per cent. in as many districts of India, and Thomas Newcome, who had plenty of money for his own wants, would never have thought of speculation. His desire was to see his boy endowed with all the possible gifts of fortune. Had he built a palace for Clive, and been informed that a roc's egg was required to complete the decoration of the edifice, Tom Newcome would have travelled to the world's end in search of the wanting article. . . . The strong and eager covet honour and enjoyment for themselves; the gentle and disappointed (once they may have been strong and eager too) desire these gifts for their children. 51

From the day that he discovers that he cannot get what he wants for his son the Colonel begins to turn bitter and to act unreasonably and Thackeray makes it clear that there has been no essential change in his nature. The narrator comments:

People hate, as they love, unreasonably. Whether is it the more mortifying to us, to feel that we are disliked or liked undeservedly? 56

In the days of his bitterness the Colonel is acting from basically the same principle as the odious Mrs. Mackenzie, the Campaigner, surely one of the most objectionable women in fiction? She is driven by the principle of selfishness acting on a mean and narrow nature. His nature is the reverse but the driving power is the same, though distanced and made obscure by the transference of his desires from himself to Clive.

The Colonel saves himself when the goodness of his nature is allowed to reassert itself after his financial ruin. His punishment is terrible and his death most pathetic. The Colonel's strength, bodily as well as mental, stems from his innocence, and Mrs. Mackenzie, after his fall, is the persistent reminder of his guilt. The Colonel withdraws from the world and dies. In a sense he had always been withdrawn from the world but by returning to Greyfriars he tries to recapture the innocence of his youth.

Even when we are most out of sympathy with the Colonel we are reminded of his truth and simplicity. During the election when he is dragged down by disappointment and bitterness there is still enough unselfish honesty in him to enable him to realise his own error. His loss of contact with Clive makes him realise that he is wrong and he cries out, 'I'm wrong—and thank God I am wrong—and God bless you, my own boy!' (Chapter 68). Other characters are saved by the reawakening of the same human qualities within them. Ethel's self-discovery follows the shock of her sister-in-law's elopement and allows her to escape from the materialistic trap into which her own superficial desires had driven her. Even old Major Pendennis, the hardened social warrior of *Pendennis*, re-emerges once more in a brief but touching death-bed repentance:

> Not many more feasts was Arthur Pendennis, senior, to have in this world. Not many more great men was he to flatter, nor schemes to wink at, nor earthly pleasures to enjoy. His long days were well nigh ended: on his last couch, which Laura tended so affectionately, with his last breath almost, he faltered out to me, 'I had other views for you, my boy, and once hoped to see you in a higher position in life; but I begin to think now, Arthur, that I was wrong; and as for that girl, sir, I'm sure she is an angel.' 49

Even Lady Kew, that other fierce old warrior, is allowed to die without being entirely condemned. We are left with no shadow of doubt that the course of life which she advocates and tries to force on those around her is a vicious one, but we are compelled to see her as in part the victim of her own training and environment. Like Beatrix in *The Virginians* she can feel at times; under the influence of her attachment to Ethel she becomes a softer character than we would at one time have thought possible. Her behaviour is not the result of malice but stems from an inbred system of values which places social distinction at the summit of human achievement. She tells Ethel: '. . . you belong to your belongings, my dear. . . .' and has an element of devotion in her creed. When she dies at last there is a good deal of pity in the narrator's final assessment of her life:

> But to live to fourscore years, and be found dancing among the idle virgins! To have had near a century of allotted time, and then be called away from the giddy notes of a Mayfair fiddle! To have to yield your roses too, and then drop out of the bony clutch of your

old fingers a wreath that came from a Parisian bandbox!....Here is
one who reposes after a long feast where no love has been; after
girlhood without kindly maternal nurture; marriage without
affection; matronhood without its precious griefs and joys; after
fourscore years of lonely vanity. Let us take off our hats to that
procession too as it passes, admiring the different lots awarded to the
children of men, and the various usages to which Heaven puts its
creatures.                                                    55

Lady Kew, sister to the Marquis of Steyne, was chief pillar and
product of the empty, meaningless aristocratic code which, in
*The Newcomes*, we see passing away.

One thing Lady Kew shared with Colonel Newcome—an
inability to think well of Clive's chosen profession; for both of
them a painter belonged to Bohemia and was committed to
lower-class life. To be a painter was to be entirely outside the
respectable world; as Hobson Newcome tells his nephew Barnes,
'. . . hang it—a painter's no trade at all. . . .' The Colonel has
respect for the arts and is prepared to consider a painter a gentleman, but he cannot overcome his consciousness of the origins of
Clive's friend and superior, J. J. Ridley:

> . . . when young Ridley and his son became pupils at Gandish's, he
> could [with difficulty] be induced to invite the former to his parties.
> 'An artist is any man's equal,' he said. 'I have no prejudice of that
> sort; and think that Sir Joshua Reynolds and Dr. Johnson were fit
> company for any person, of whatever rank. But a young man whose
> father may have had to wait behind me at dinner, should not be
> brought into my company.' Clive compromises the dispute with a
> laugh. 'First,' says he, 'I will wait till I am asked; and then I promise
> I will not go to dine with Lord Todmorden.'                    19

This attitude indicates a weakness on the Colonel's part and a lack
of awareness of the importance of painting in his son's life.
Thackeray makes sure that his readers are aware of it, mainly
through J. J. Ridley, the only character in the novel who fulfils
the conditions for happiness suggested at the end of *Vanity Fair*—
he has his desire and is satisfied with it. Through his devotion to
his art, Ridley frees himself from self-consciousness and from the

world. Pendennis makes a pointed comparison between Ridley and Clive:

> The painter turned as he spoke; and the bright northern light which fell upon the sitter's head was intercepted, and lighted up his own as he addressed us. Out of that bright light looked his pale thoughtful face, and long locks, and eager brown eyes. . . . Occupied over that consoling work, idle thoughts cannot gain the mastery over him; selfish wishes or desires are kept at bay. Art is truth: and truth is religion; and its study and practice a daily work of pious duty. What are the world's struggles, brawls, successes, to that calm recluse pursuing his calling? . . . . What know you of his art? You cannot read the alphabet of that sacred book, good old Thomas Newcome! What can you tell of its glories, joys, secrets, consolations? Between his two best-beloved mistresses, poor Clive's luckless father somehow interposes; and with sorrowful, even angry protests. In place of Art the Colonel brings him a ledger; and in lieu of first love, shows him Rosey. 65

Thackeray is not putting forward Ridley's idealistic devotion to Art as the pattern of human conduct. Ridley's love makes him withdraw from the world while people like Clive find their salvation within it. What is important about the passage above is that it reflects Thackeray's conviction that people can only live with a chance of happiness by finding a relationship outside themselves, with a person or an object which is congenial to them. Devotion to Mammon, the God of respectable society, is destructive and leads to unhappiness because it involves a denial of human feeling, bringing the individual in the end to hollowness and loneliness. Lady Kew and Sir Barnes Newcome, though for somewhat different reasons, devote themselves to materialism, and both suffer in their development as people. Others, like the Newcome brothers and their wives, preserve some of their humanity but are emotionally stunted. Some, like Charles Honeyman and Frederick Bayham, escape selfishness and become able to live according to their better qualities rather than their worse.

The ending of *The Newcomes* has been compared to that of *Great Expectations* because both novels were altered in order to permit of marriage between the respective heroes and heroines. The comparison is not entirely fair. Readers object to *Great Expectations* on the grounds that the ending suggests a marriage which the character development within the novel makes unlikely. This is not the case with *The Newcomes*. Thackeray was aware that his decision to allow Clive and Ethel to marry meant that he had to hurry Rosey off the scene in rather an undignified and casual manner, but that was all he had to do. He had prepared for the ending by showing the gradual deepening of the original attraction which they had for each other and had removed the obstacles to their union when he brought Ethel to realise the evil effects of inhibiting natural love for the sake of materialistic ends. Rosey's death is not implausible because it is, in a sense, the result of the lack of life which is what makes her so totally unsuitable as a wife for Clive. Then, the possibility of the marriage is part of the general feeling of hope and promise which pervades the ending of this otherwise melancholy novel. The death of Colonel Newcome has been rightly compared to that of King Lear in so far as it is the natural if painful result of age and exhaustion brought about by extravagant emotional commitment. It is similar also in that it leaves us with a sense of completeness and allows us to feel some hope for a continuation of social life. The Colonel's death is not tragic, but it is full of pathos and sentiment. He dies as a child rather than a man, returning to the loneliness of his boyhood from the much crueller loneliness of his age. He leaves behind him a wider group of relationships, a larger number of human beings connected by love for him and for each other, than had existed at any time during the course of the novel. His death is accompanied by the prayers of the woman he had loved throughout his life, and the reader has a sense that with him dies the old divisive world in which he had suffered.

# 8

# Later Works

The later part of Thackeray's career as a creative writer cannot be considered apart from his position as editor of the *Cornhill Magazine*. Ever since he finished *Esmond* he had been thinking of giving himself a fallow period during which he should not write novels. The success of *The Newcomes*, which brought his reputation to its highest point, diverted his mind from fears of sterility for a while, but the failure of *The Virginians*, which was not a financial success, made him think again in terms of a prolonged rest. Then in February 1859 he received a proposal from George Smith, head of the rising house of Smith, Elder, for a novel to be published in parts. This proposal, which was too generous to resist, was followed in April by a further proposal that Thackeray should undertake the editorship of the projected *Cornhill Magazine* at an annual salary of £1,000. Acceptance of these proposals forced Thackeray back into the pattern of intense creative activity complicated by the burden of critical and editorial duties; and until 1862, when he resigned the editorship, the idea of a period of rest was put aside.

The success of the *Cornhill Magazine* was greater than the wildest hopes of editor or publisher. The first number sold 120,000 copies and the average for the next six was 85,000; and George Smith generously raised the editor's salary to £2,000. With this and the £350 which Thackeray received for each part of the serials which he wrote for the magazine, added to the twelve guineas which he received for each page of miscellaneous material he contributed, he had an income of £7,000. The first thing Thackeray did with the money was to start building a house in the style of Queen Anne, which he completed in March 1862. The process of planning, building and furnishing this house gave him enormous satisfaction; when finished it was the kind of home which he had always wanted. However, these last years of his life, though the most prosperous by far, brought him neither peace of mind nor quietness. In 1858 the worsening relations between himself and Dickens had come to a head in the affair which followed the publication of an insulting article on Thackeray in a very minor magazine by an equally minor journalist, Edmund Yates. Thackeray was annoyed because he thought that the information used in the article could only have been gained as a result of Yates's membership of the Garrick Club, and he laid the matter before its committee. Yates was expelled, parties formed and feelings ran high, while behind Yates stood Dickens, giving advice and direction on the conduct of the anti-Garrick and anti-Thackeray campaign.

The trouble which this incident caused Thackeray went on until the end of his life. In 1863 he and Dickens met and a reconciliation took place, but the separation between the two men could never be healed. With his editorship of the *Cornhill* Thackeray stood at the head of one part of the literary world, increasingly identified with cynicism and conservatism by his enemies, who harassed him by attacks on his work and personality and on that of his daughter, who began her own career as a novelist in May 1860. Only a few months before his death, the founding of the National Shakespeare Tercentenary Celebratory Committee was made the occasion for an attack on him by two of his less significant opponents. Meanwhile, throughout the period from 1860 the attacks of ill health which had always attended him increased in frequency and began to wear him down. The almost compulsive habits of eating and drinking from which he never freed himself finally had their effect, and on the morning of 24 December 1863, he was discovered dead in his bed.

'LOVEL THE WIDOWER'

The first contribution Thackeray made to the *Cornhill Magazine* was a long story, *Lovel the Widower*. This was a reworking of a play which Thackeray had written as early as 1854 but which had been rejected by the two London managers to whom he submitted it and which had taken up the characters used four years before that, in *The Kickleburys on the Rhine*. The play, *The Wolves and the Lamb*, does not lack dramatic quality but it fails as a play because it depends too much on explanation in dialogue and static scenes rather than consecutive action. When he reworked it as *Lovel the Widower* he took the figure of Captain Touchit, merely an observer in the play, and changed him into Mr. Bachelor, the narrator, involving him more closely with the action. The result is interesting for what it can tell us about Thackeray's technique, though it has never been popular with readers. The basic situation is indicated in the title of the play: the lamb is a governess in the house of a widower who is dominated by his mother and mother-in-law; at the same time the lamb is the widower, at the mercy of the three women. In the play the main focus rests on the governess, who is forced into deceit and moral compromise in order to maintain her position, and the dramatic climax comes with her unmasking by the mothers and the sudden declaration of love by Lovel. The plot of the story is much more complex, and the focal point is shifted. Thackeray keeps the situation as it was in the play but adds the personality of the narrator, the weak, self-centred but good-natured Mr. Bachelor, and he gives us a great deal of information about the background of the heroine. At the same time he alters the governess's situation so as to throw a great deal of doubt on the degree to which she has been unaffected by the life which she has been forced to lead, adding to the dramatic scene of discovery the psychological drama through which the narrator has to pass, loving the governess but too fastidious to trust her. The moral tone of the piece is complex and not pleasant; the strong and effective comedy and the subtly humorous use of symbol make the story interesting, but the degree to which our sympathy with the central characters is deliberately impaired weakens its impact.

'THE ADVENTURES OF PHILIP'

*Lovel the Widower* was not popular with the readers of the

*Cornhill Magazine*, but *The Adventures of Philip*, which appeared between January 1861 and August 1862, met with more success. Even so, the novel has no claim to be considered among Thackeray's major works. It contains some of his most effective writing but goes over the same ground that he had already covered in *Pendennis*, dealing with the growth and the misfortunes of a young man. *The Adventures of Philip* repays study if only because it is the most autobiographical of Thackeray's novels, but it is not of major interest. The character of the hero is not particularly appealing, and although some of the minor characters are vividly portrayed the novel as a whole never comes to life.

Like *Lovel the Widower*, *The Adventures of Philip* grew out of something which Thackeray had written earlier in his career—it takes up the story of *A Shabby Genteel Story*, which he had written twenty years before. In the interval the characters had lost some of their interest. Caroline Gan, now the deserted wife of Brandon (renamed Dr. Brand Firmin), is a pathetic and appealing character and Thackeray's treatment of her is frequently impressive—as in the dramatic scene when she overcomes the brutalised Hunt with the help of a cupboard door and a bottle of ether. But Caroline Gan and the equally impressive hypocrite, Dr. Brand Firmin, are not strong enough to compensate for the weakness of the central character. Philip Firmin has none of the interest of Clive Newcome nor the charm of Arthur Pendennis and the reader finds it difficult to accept without such compensation the rather stupid pride and physical aggressiveness which are his main characteristics. It is difficult to share the excitement of the ending, even though it is Thackeray's most sensational dénouement because by the time that it comes the reader has ceased to wish for anything but the end of the book.

THE 'ROUNDABOUT PAPERS'

While Thackeray was editing the *Cornhill* and contributing the monthly parts of *Lovel the Widower* and *The Adventures of Philip*, and even after he had ceased to edit the magazine, he was regularly publishing a series of *Roundabout Papers* which are, in their own way, among the most interesting things that he wrote. *The Adventures of Philip*, where for the first time in his career the author seems to lose control of his digressive commentary, would make it appear that Thackeray had lost the novel writer's ability to keep his material under formal control and that these discursive papers were the natural end to his career. Yet right at the very end of his life Thackeray was busy with a novel which was unfinished at his death and which proves that he still had the power of formal control shown in *Esmond*. The three chapters of this novel, *Denis Duval*, which he had time to write were published in the *Cornhill Magazine* after his death and prove conclusively that Thackeray never lost the novelist's art of assimilating his material and giving it objective form. The narrator, Denis Duval himself, who, like Barry Lyndon and Henry Esmond, tells his own story, shares with previous hero-narrators only his vividness and is as triumphantly an individual as they ever were.

Nevertheless, the *Roundabout Papers* did give Thackerary an opportunity to exploit his peculiar gifts, allowing him to write freely on topics of the day and subjects which occurred to him at random, giving free play to his imagination, his attraction to anecdote and reminiscence. The source of artistic control in them seems to be a finely-developed sense of discretion and appropriateness. George Saintsbury wrote of them:

> To me the *Roundabout Papers* are almost as much a whole, a microcosm, as many celebrated books of great writers composed nominally on a single theme: but of course they are individual wholes as well. And their individuality, so to speak, 'promiscuous', prevented that appearance of the desultory which, though it far exceeds the reality, is charged against his larger works.
>
> INTRODUCTION TO THE OXFORD THACKERAY XVII, xv

The 'promiscuousness' and the unity of each and all of these essays are immediately apparent. With a brilliantly simple style Thackeray combined fantasy and realism, freeing himself to pass through space and time. The detail of his technique is basically similar to that in the novels, illustrated by sentences like the following:

> I would as soon have believed that a promissory note of Sir John Falstaff (accepted by Messrs. Bardolph and Nym, and payable in Aldgate) would be as sure to find payment, as that note of the departed—nay, lamented—Jack Thriftless.
>
> ON A MEDAL OF GEORGE THE FOURTH

Characters from Shakespeare, from Swift, from the whole range of English literature, from the *Arabian Nights*, from Rome or Greece, from the 14th century, the 18th or the 19th, are created anew and fixed in place with realistic detail and pointed wit. Through each paper runs a vein of airy fantasy which surprises by its appropriateness and encourages the reader to trust himself to the wayward and appealing logic of the essayist.

*On some Carp at Sans Souci* is a good example of a *Roundabout Paper*, showing the characteristics of style and structure which are common to them all. The fixed point of reference is the old woman, Goody Twoshoes, an inhabitant of the workhouse whom the author has befriended and entertained. She is ninety years old, decrepit, senile, small-minded, almost subhuman in the limitation of her mental activity, having none of the dignity of age. At this stage in the paper there is no apparent connection between Goody Twoshoes and the Carp in the pond at Sans Souci in Potsdam, and it is part of the nature of these papers that there should be tension between the apparent unconnected-ness and the reader's desire to perceive the connection, which is satisfied only at the end. From the old woman's senile cares the essayist moves back through English history, linking her with Marlborough, Sterne, Goldsmith, the Great Exhibition of 1851, returning from this excursion with renewed awareness of the meaninglessness of her age:

> 'Don't talk to me your nonsense about Exhibitions, and Prince Dukes, and toads in coals, or coals in toads, or what is it?' says Granny. 'I know there was a good Queen Charlotte, for she left me snuff; and it comforts me of a night when I lie awake.'

From the childishness of the old woman, who now cares for

nothing but the most immediate and trivial, the author moves in imagination to the days when she might have felt something and, again, from the transience of her youth to reminiscence of his own and the element of human affection which has now left him. Human affection dies away out of his mind and leaves behind it trivial selfishness, the realism of age; and at this point only we are ready for the Carp at Sans Souci:

Those eyes may have goggled from beneath the weeds at Napoleon's jack-boots; they have seen Frederick's lean shanks reflected in their pool; and perhaps Monsieur de Voltaire has fed them—and now, for a crumb of biscuit they will fight, push, hustle, rob, squabble, gobble, relapsing into their tranquillity when the ignoble struggle is over. Sans souci, indeed!

# Conclusion

The end of this essay, *On Some Carp at Sans Souci*, returns us, tacitly, to the fact of kindness. The paper is sentimental and satirical. It is an uncompromising destruction of all the illusions we have about human dignity in age. The picture of the old women in the workhouse and the carp in the pool, sharply realised and concretely realistic, is yet qualified by the tone of the narrator's voice, modified by the essentially human and refined meditation. This paper and the many like it which Thackeray wrote towards the end of his life is the most restrained and mellow of his writings, and different from anything else he did. Yet in the *Roundabout Papers* are present the same elements which make up his novels and tales, elements which were always being forced into new patterns though never essentially changed.

In all Thackeray's mature writing we see an unfailing ability to create an impression of life, but this ability is always accompanied by a tendency to generalise from the concrete example. His career as a writer shows an early effort to define his own attitudes and to achieve maturity of handling and control over his material. Once these qualities had been achieved, the effort was replaced by an attempt to balance against each other the opposing aspects of his art, satire and sentiment, realism and abstract meditation. He worked best when he was working with small units, and his work is full of paragraphs, even sentences, which can be taken as epitomes of his technique. For this reason he was suited to the system of publishing in numbers, and with *Vanity Fair* and *The Newcomes* he achieved a perfect balance of the elements which make up his art. With *Esmond* he succeeded in writing a novel which was composed as a whole, but its unity does not depend on a story; it is a unity of tone derived from the character of the narrator. Both *Pendennis* and *The Virginians* are important novels, containing striking and unforgettable incidents and characters—the former, furthermore, is one of the major records of Victorian sensibility. But both these novels are structurally weak, superficially dependent on a story plot which conflicts with other aims of the novelist.

Thackeray more than any other English writer of the 19th century set out to create a 'world' which runs parallel to the real world which he is apparently describing. After *Vanity Fair* he began to build up, by a system of cross references, a full and detailed social world of his own, using minor characters from an early work as major characters in later stories, returning for the plots of new novels to family history hinted at in previous ones. It is not by chance that he makes Barry Lyndon reappear in the pages of *The Virginians* or scatters stray facts about the Crawley family through his later work. In *Esmond*, *The Virginians* and *Pendennis* he traces the history of one family and through them of a society. His work as a whole presents a considered appraisal of English social history from 1690 to 1863, while within the compass of the individual novel there are repeated movements back and fore in time. By his portrayal of social history he was able to show the development of a code of behaviour and morality and to contrast it with that which was predominant in other times. Considered as a whole his work is a massive and massively impressive statement of the creed which finds its expression separately in each novel.

With great creative power Thackeray achieved a degree of vividness and drama which at times demands and receives the reader's total emotional involvement. There are scenes and characters in Thackeray's work which can never be forgotten and which have not been excelled by any other writer. At the same time he keeps a distance between his characters and his readers, forces the latter to be aware of the difference between illusion and reality, the past of action and the present of narration, and attains a unique range of effect and implication. Critics have spoken much in recent years in terms of a simple distinction between 'telling' and 'showing' as methods of narrating a story, and much derogatory criticism of Thackeray has resulted from the application of these terms. Yet if such a distinction is useful for the treatment of some novelists—and that is open to doubt—it is certainly inappropriate where Thackeray is concerned. The dramatic incidents in Thackeray's novels are inseparable from the so-called 'commentary', are part of the same unit of prose, the same chapter and the same number. Of all the forms of narration he employs, the first person, autobiographical, is the most frequent. The earlier part of his career is a history of constant experimentation with different *personae* and uses of *personae*. Even his omniscient narrator is a person in his own right, changing his qualities at the will of the author and always distinct from him. These facts are significant: they indicate that Thackeray was not concerned to create an 'illusion of life' so much as to achieve subtlety of meaning and that he used his superb creative ability not merely to involve the reader emotionally but to interest and intrigue him and to control and direct his attention to the various implications of the shifting texture of realised life.

## THACKERAY AND THE CRITICS

During and for some time after his lifetime Thackeray was well treated by the critics. In the frequent comparisons which were made between him and Dickens it was pointed out that he was a different type of writer who shared none of his rival's faults and had many distinct and remarkable virtues of his own. At this time it was recognised that his contribution in turning the Victorian novel towards realism was decisive and he was thought of as being the spearhead of the movement which at once expanded the range of the novel and bound it inextricably to the terms of ordinary life. Many critics objected to what they called his cynicism, his sordid view of the world, but as he remarked himself about a reviewer in *The Times* (see p. 97), such people were unaware of what he was trying to do. At the basis of his approach to the novel was a revulsion from the vapourings, from what George Meredith called the 'headless and tail-less imaginings', of the idealistic novel, and a determination to press home his statement that sentimentalism or idealisation in literature could only lead to falsity. In this matter he disagreed with Dickens, finding his art, the art of exaggeration and caricature, unnatural and therefore false.

Many of Thackeray's contemporaries agreed with him in his opinion of Dickens and many more found the more prolific and boisterous writer vulgar, sentimental and clumsy in his approach to the subjects which he chose to treat. In Victorian England the tendency was, among intellectuals at least, for Thackeray to be spoken of as the superior writer. After their death both underwent radical reassessment and their popularity gave way before that of their successors. In the 20th century one of them has again been elevated to major status and hailed as a great novelist. The other has not been ignored and is steadily increasing his reputation, but the difference in their treatment has been drastic and the disparity remains striking.

To account for this difference in treatment simply in terms of a difference in quality would be to fall into the mistake of reflecting literary fashions. In fact the literary fashions which have dictated the terms in which Dickens has been praised have prevented the proper assessment of Thackeray's work. Dickens's novels can easily be discussed in term of formal unity and 'organic' structure; they lean heavily on symbol and metaphor, both of which are attractive to the 20th-century critic. Many of them can be easily approached by the critic who is looking for earnestness of purpose while others lend themselves to the type of criticism concerned to find archetypal or 'mythic' patterns. Dickens's career as an artist shows him increasingly concerned with an analysis of the position of the individual with regard to social and moral values which is in harmony with prominent elements in modern thought.

On the other hand, Thackeray outrages the critical standards based on a qualitative distinction between 'telling' and 'showing'; his use of language is subtle rather than vigorous, allusive rather than dramatic. Thackeray openly rejected the kind of moral earnestness which Dickens proclaimed and in his social satire came down on the side of restraint and adjustment, assuming that social life imposes certain conditions on the individual. As a result of these characteristics there has been a tendency for critics to dismiss him as a writer who could create characters but who has nothing to say to modern man about the 'human condition'. Any detailed study of Thackeray's work reveals his essential seriousness and proves his importance as a novelist. How important he is it is impossible to say until more detailed work has been done and the alteration of the critical climate has proceeded farther than it has yet.

Meanwhile it is necessary to realise that reading Thackeray is not a simple activity but a demanding one. A Thackeray novel does not draw the reader in to an illusory world but asks him to take part in a process of discovery. The tone of his work is subtle and strangely elusive, dependent ultimately on the texture of his style and the manipulation of the narrator. Time has shown that Walter Bagehot was too hopeful about how soon it would be possible to make a final assessment of Thackeray's status. In 1867 he said:

> When the young critics of this year have gray hairs, their children will tell them what is the judgment of posterity upon Mr. Thackeray. STERNE AND THACKERAY

By now we may suspect that such a judgment will never come, that the subtlety and richness of his work must become increasingly apparent but that it will remains for each generation to define its attitude to Thackeray rather than to judge him. To some readers irritating, to others fascinating, Thackeray must remain what his contemporaries thought him—a great writer and perhaps among the greatest.

# Bibliography

The most authoritative account of Thackeray's life is the two-volume biography by G. N. Ray: *Thackeray. The Uses of Adversity, 1811–1846*, 1955, and *Thackeray. The Age of Wisdom, 1847–1863*, published by Oxford Univ. Press, 1958. The most comprehensive edition of the letters is also edited by G. N. Ray, in four volumes: *The Letters and Private Papers of William Makepeace Thackeray*, Oxford Univ. Press, 1945–6.

Very little modern criticism of Thackeray exists in book form, but the most useful volumes recently produced are: G. Tillotson, *Thackeray the Novelist*, Cambridge Univ. Press, 1954 and University Paperbacks, 1963; and J. Loofbourouw, *Thackeray and the Form of Fiction*, Princeton Univ. Press, 1964.

There are no modern editions of Thackeray's complete works, although the edition of *Vanity Fair* published by Methuen in 1963 (edited by K. and G. Tillotson) is excellent. Of older editions the Smith, Elder *Biographical Edition*, 1898–9, is unique in containing the biographical prefaces written by Thackeray's daughter, while the *Oxford Edition* of 1919 has excellent critical introductions by G. Saintsbury and is more complete.

Other books referred to in the course of this study are: D. Cecil, *Early Victorian Novelists*, Constable, 1934; K. Tillotson, *Novels of the Eighteen-Forties*, Oxford Univ. Press, 1954; D. Van Ghent, *The English Novel Form and Function*, Rhinehart, 1953; J. Butt and K. Tillotson, *Dickens at Work*, Methuen, 1957.

# Index